CLEAR WRITING

A Step-by-Step Guide

Diana Bonet

A FIFTY-MINUTE™ SERIES BOOK

CRISP PUBLICATIONS, INC.
Menlo Park, California

CLEAR WRITING
A Step-by-Step Guide

Diana Bonet

CREDITS
Editor: **Elaine Brett**
Layout and Composition: **Interface Studio**
Cover Design: **Carol Harris**
Artwork: **Jeff Mockus**

Copyright © 1991 by Crisp Publications, Inc.
Printed in the United States of America

English language Crisp books are distributed worldwide. Our major international distributors include:

CANADA: Reid Publishing Ltd., Box 69559—109 Thomas St., Oakville, Ontario, Canada L6J 7R4. TEL: (905) 842-4428, FAX: (905) 842-9327

Raincoast Books Distribution Ltd., 112 East 3rd Avenue, Vancouver, British Columbia, Canada V5T 1C8. TEL: (604) 873-6581, FAX: (604) 874-2711

AUSTRALIA: Career Builders, P.O. Box 1051, Springwood, Brisbane, Queensland, Australia 4127. TEL: 841-1061, FAX: 841-1580

NEW ZEALAND: Career Builders, P.O. Box 571, Manurewa, Auckland, New Zealand. TEL: 266-5276, FAX: 266-4152

JAPAN: Phoenix Associates Co., Mizuho Bldg. 2-12-2, Kami Osaki, Shinagawa-Ku, Tokyo 141, Japan. TEL: 3-443-7231, FAX: 3-443-7640

Selected Crisp titles are also available in other languages. Contact International Rights Manager Suzanne Kelly at (415) 323-6100 for more information.

Library of Congress Catalog Card Number 90-84924
Bonet, Diana
Clear Writing: A Step-by-Step Guide
ISBN 1-56052-094-9

This book is printed on recyclable paper with soy ink.

PREFACE

Clear writing is a step-by-step process. This book is designed to teach you to write basic business letters and memos—one step at a time. In fact, it teaches you the basic steps in writing *anything*—one step at a time. *Clear Writing* provides an easy-to-follow formula to help you write clearly, in complete sentences. Once you learn the formula, you can always write clearly. Each step builds on the previous step, and there are many examples to help you understand the step you are mastering. At first you work with nouns and verbs, then short, easy sentences. You practice each step until you have mastered it. Then you tackle longer sentences. Move through the book at your own pace. As you work through the steps, the correct answers are always at the end of the section. This method helps you gain confidence as you gain skill. You will learn what to say and how to say it in a way that helps your reader understand your meaning.

Clear writing is possible for everyone. If writing is difficult for you because English is your second language or you did not complete high school, this book offers real help. If you did not understand all the fuss about nouns and verbs in English class, you will find help here. Or if you just want more work with basic writing skills, this book will be very useful. If you stay with it and commit yourself to the task, you can improve your present writing skills. Users of this formula have been shown to improve their writing skills by more than fifty percent, based on the SEEK Index developed by Diana Bonet and Alan Cohen.

Clear writing is not difficult. You need to know only a few rules in order to write well. This book contains the most important rules and shows you how to use them. For complete information on spelling, punctuation, and special problems with English as a second language, refer to Jack Swenson's companion book, *The Building Blocks of Business Writing*.

Clear writing is important. You can improve your image, get a better job, and earn more money if you write well. You also save time and money for your company, and create good relations with your coworkers and customers. Good writing tells your readers that you are thinking clearly. It gives them confidence in you.

We hope you enjoy *Clear Writing* and find it useful. Writing can change from a boring job to a pleasant task, and with your new skills you might even find that writing is fun. Anything is possible! Grab your pencil and let's get started.

ACKNOWLEDGMENTS

I wish to thank the following people for making this book possible. Without them I could not have written it. Nor would I have as much love, learning, and laughter in my life. I thank Gary Romero for his encouragement, his love, and his eye for detail. Don Ricks originated many of the ideas that evolved into CORE CONTROL©, the formula used in this book. He was my mentor and my friend. Harold Hadden has supported me in every way as an investor in my future, and as my friend. Thanks to Jack Swenson, my copartner in this book, for his help and confidence in our project. My dear friends Lisette Wilbur, Stevie and Richard Doughty, Ken and Toni Fratzke, Suzie Hilgeman, and all of the Wings have encouraged me and helped me keep my sense of humor. Ashleigh Brilliant is heavily quoted in the examples and exercises. I thank him for his wacky wit and wisdom. Finally, I want to thank my publisher, Mike Crisp. No one could ask for a more flexible, positive person in the driver's seat.

CONTENTS

PLEASE START HERE...
AN INTRODUCTION TO
CORE CONTROL

In the preface you read that we are using a formula to learn basic business writing skills. Picture in your mind some crazed English professor busily stirring beakers of strange chemicals to create a magic formula for clear writing. By dipping our pens in the formula, we suddenly become the Shakespeares of business writing. Why can't writing be that easy? Perhaps it can. Almost.

The writing formula you will learn in this book will make your writing tasks much easier. By formula, we mean that every sentence has a pattern that is similar in all sentences. This pattern is so much the same in every sentence that we can always depend on it. From this basic pattern, we have created an easy-to-follow formula called CORE CONTROL. In the beginning of the book you will be introduced to the nouns and verbs that make up this CORE CONTROL formula. Starting with the noun-verb formula, you will practice writing short, clear, complete sentences. Then you will write longer sentences, then paragraphs, and finally, complete letters, memos, and essays.

The noun-verb formula is based on the idea that the subject (a noun) and the verb form the core of any sentence. Sentence cores are like apple cores because they both contain seeds. In writing, the core of the sentence is the noun and the verb. These are the seeds from which sentences grow. The core is the most important part of the sentence. Without a subject and a verb (the core), we do not have a complete sentence. When you are consciously choosing the nouns and verbs that make up the core, you are using CORE CONTROL. This book shows you how to choose the right words, why you should choose them, and how they help you write more clearly.

To better understand what a sentence is and what it does, let's begin by studying the complete and incomplete sentences on the next page.

SECTION 1

SENTENCE BASICS

WHAT IS A SENTENCE?

A sentence is a group of words that make sense when used together. A sentence expresses a complete thought. *If a sentence does not express a complete thought, it is an incomplete sentence.* A sentence begins with a capital letter and ends with a period(.), an exclamation point(!), or a question mark(?). Every sentence has a **subject** and a **verb**. Sentences are the basic units of all writing. Below you will see examples of incomplete sentences and complete sentences.

EXAMPLES

Incomplete Sentences

1. When we left the house at three o'clock.
2. Joining the Army when he was seventeen.
3. As I reached for the peanut butter.
4. That her desk was on fire.
5. About incomplete sentences.

The sentences above are incomplete because they do not express complete ideas. They express only parts of ideas, and you are left wondering what happened.

Complete Sentences

1. We left the house at three o'clock.
2. He joined the Army when he was seventeen.
3. I reached for the peanut butter.
4. No one noticed that her desk was on fire.
5. We will learn about incomplete sentences.

These sentences express complete ideas. Each idea is followed by a period to show that it is a complete thought.

4

EXERCISE FOR PRACTICE

In the following exercise, put a C next to each complete sentence and an I next to each incomplete sentence. Even though these sentences are punctuated, they may not be complete sentences. When you have finished the exercise, check your answers at the end of this section.

_____ 1. At our new offices on Main Street.

_____ 2. Really funny, but serious too.

_____ 3. Mr. Firbaugh's expense account is late again.

_____ 4. When I exercise, especially after work.

_____ 5. Tom stood there biting his nails.

_____ 6. But only when she wasn't looking.

_____ 7. Will I win if I buy a ticket?

_____ 8. Because he was boring!

_____ 9. Time flies.

_____ 10. For anyone who is concerned about money.

FINDING THE SUBJECT OF A SENTENCE

To write well, we must understand the different parts of a sentence. When we understand the parts, we can control our writing more easily. The most important word in a sentence is the **subject**. Every sentence has a subject. The subject is the topic of the sentence. It is often one word, and it is usually found near the beginning of the sentence. It tells you *who* or *what* the sentence is about. The subject is usually a noun or a pronoun. A **noun** is a person, place, or thing. A **pronoun** is a word like *I*, *he*, or *you* that takes the place of a noun. Nouns and pronouns are used most often as subjects of sentences. For example,

John moved the copier. *John* is a noun.

He moved the copier. *He* is a pronoun that takes the place of the word *John*.

EXAMPLES

My *neighbor* waxes her garden hose.
Cleo makes the best chili in town.
We delivered the machine parts to the warehouse.
The *monkeys* looked puzzled when the boy ate the banana.
The *rain* fell harder and harder.

EXERCISE FOR PRACTICE

Underline the subject of each sentence in the following sentences. When you have finished, check your answers at the end of this section.

1. She completed the test in ten minutes.
2. The Browns live next door.
3. Alice and Albert broke the lock on the old trunk.
4. The doors to the office were jammed.
5. Have you seen my manager?
6. Few forgive without a fuss.
7. We anchored the boat and jumped overboard to swim.
8. The billing went out yesterday.
9. They can't start the meeting without us.
10. Two fire engines raced through the parking lot.

GETTING CONTROL OF THE SUBJECT

The **subject** of the sentence tells the reader who or what the sentence is about. It is the main topic of the sentence. In this sentence,

Birdwatchers are cheep dates.

Birdwatchers is the subject, because it is the word in the sentence that tells you the topic of the sentence.

The subject of a sentence is part of the sentence core. The complete core is the subject, the verb, and the completer. (We will study each part of the core separately in this book.) To write clear sentences, you must control the subject. When you control the subject, you are in charge of what your reader sees and understands. To help your readers, give them a ''picture word'' as a subject. A picture word creates a clear picture of an object or a person in your reader's mind.

EXAMPLES

My manager arrives early. *Manager* is the subject. Can you see a picture of your manager in your mind?

The boxes came without lids. *Boxes* is the subject. Can you see a picture of boxes in your mind?

Because your reader sees pictures when you give a visual cue, you can control the subject of a sentence by choosing a concrete noun (we call it a **seed noun**) as a subject. You help your reader ''see'' what you are saying. Seed nouns paint pictures in people's minds.

Seed nouns name *people* or *things* or *places* just as concrete nouns do. Some examples of seed nouns are: *telephone, engine, football,* and *Elvis Presley.* The pronouns *I, you, he, she, it, we, you* (plural), and *they* are seed nouns, because they substitute for seed nouns; for example, in *"I paid the invoice,"* I is considered a seed noun. Seed nouns have substance (you can touch them) and they occupy space (like the Starship *Enterprise*). The old saying "A picture is worth a thousand words" is true for sentence subjects.

Use seed nouns (visual words) as subjects of sentences in at least eighty percent of the sentences that you write. By doing so, you control the core of your sentence, because the subject is the key to any sentence.

EXERCISE FOR PRACTICE

In the following sentences <u>underline</u> the seed nouns or pronouns that are used as subjects. Do not underline subjects that are not seed nouns or pronouns. You may find other seed nouns or pronouns within a sentence. Do not bother to underline them; stay focused on sentence subjects. Circle the subjects that are not seed nouns. When you have completed the exercise, check the end of this section for the answers.

EXAMPLES

<u>Charles</u> rides well.

(Anything) is good if it's made of chocolate.

The <u>books</u> disappeared.

1. Alfredo is happy with the results.
2. Four walls fell during the earthquake.
3. The team leader won an award.
4. One method involves beating the bushes.
5. Commitment is important.
6. Two bears robbed our campsite.
7. Big problems faced the crew.
8. The right answer isn't always the best answer.
9. Magicians are a vanishing breed.
10. Work is about as much fun as you make it.
11. Sinbad parked on the lawn.
12. If at first you don't succeed, you are like the rest of us.
13. The lunch room is serving bean salad.
14. At midnight the bells chimed wildly.
15. The blame was traced to the computer.

EXERCISE FOR PRACTICE

Some of the following words are seed nouns or pronouns, others are not. Underline the words that name seed nouns.

1. Goldilocks
2. for
3. quality
4. computer
5. guests
6. gently

7. programmer
8. temper
9. we
10. telephone
11. clouds
12. jogging

Write four seed nouns or pronouns of your own in the blanks provided. When you have completed these two exercises, turn to the end of this section to review the answers.

_____   _____

_____   _____

VERBS THAT WORK

In the previous section you practiced using seed nouns as sentence subjects. The seed noun is the most important part of a sentence core. The second most important part of a sentence core is the verb. In a sentence, seed nouns are followed by verbs. A **verb** tells you: (1) what the seed noun (the subject) is doing; or (2) the condition of the subject; or (3) what action is being done to the seed noun (subject). There are three kinds of verbs: **active**, **linking** and **passive**.

Active Verbs

Here is an example of a sentence that contains an active verb:

Oaks grow in the meadow.
   Oaks is the subject, *grow* is the verb that tells you what the oaks do, or what action the oaks perform. *Grow* is an active verb.

When we say that it is an active verb, we mean that the subject of the sentence is doing the acting.

OTHER EXAMPLES

Bainbreath *adjusted* the invoice.
   Bainbreath is the subject of the sentence. He is the one doing the adjusting. Adjusted is the active verb.

Jules *studied* for the exam until midnight.
   Jules (the subject of the sentence) is the one who studied until midnight. Therefore, *Jules* is the subject of the sentence. Studied is the active verb.

Our manager *hired* two new programmers.
   Our *manager* (the subject of the sentence) was the one who hired the programmers. Hired is the active verb.

EXERCISE FOR PRACTICE

In the following sentences, underline the subject with <u>one line</u> and the active verb with <u>two lines</u>. When you complete the exercise, check the end of this section for the answers.

EXAMPLES

<u>Sir Giles</u> <u>smiled</u> at the dragon.

<u>We</u> <u>built</u> a large fire.

Some <u>people</u> really <u>eat</u> brussels sprouts.

Our <u>organization</u> <u>supports</u> recycling.

1. Maryloubeth laughed at the natives.
2. Regis lives in Toledo.
3. Our manager believes that quality is important.
4. Billbob's team focuses on teamwork.
5. The security guard locked the gate.
6. She guards his delicate secret.
7. A Japanese guest toured our office.
8. They left.
9. Spotty barked at the mail carrier.
10. The concert ended.

Verb Phrases

In the previous exercise, each active verb was expressed in a single word: *laughed, lives, believes,* etc. Although some active verbs are expressed with one word, most are expressed with more than one word.

EXAMPLE

Regis *is living* in Toledo.
> *Living* is the active verb, and *is* is a **helping verb**.

The active verb and the helping verb form a **verb phrase**. Helping verbs help active verbs express the tense (time) of the verb. Following is a list of helping verbs. They are forms of the verb *to be: am, are, is, was, were, be, being, been.* Other words and phrases that you might see as part of a verb phrase include: *have, has, had, do, does, used to, going to, about to, ought to, did, doing, may, might, must, can, could, has to, have to, had to, shall, will, should, would, will be.*

In the following sentence, the verb phrase contains four words:

He *will have been attending* the class.
> The words *will have been* are helping verbs. *Attending* is the active verb. The complete verb phrase is: *will have been attending*.

OTHER EXAMPLES

We *ought to be going*.
Ezra *has been riding* horses for years.
I *must sell* my car.
The company *will be asked* for a donation.

EXERCISE FOR PRACTICE

In the following exercise, underline the subject with <u>one line</u> and the complete verb phrase with <u>two lines</u>. Check your answers at the end of this section.

EXAMPLES

The <u>puppy</u> <u>was swimming</u> in the lake.

Our <u>team</u> <u>is leading</u> the race.

His <u>department</u> <u>has been releasing</u> the parts too slowly.

1. Birdie should receive the award.
2. Jeeves will show you to the door.
3. Mrs. Turtletaub has given me another chance.
4. The training director is announcing the new class schedule.
5. Our secretary will be routing the memo through your office.
6. We have told him everything.
7. The auditors will be completing their work early.
8. The furnace is behaving strangely.
9. The committee is giving sweatshirts as prizes.
10. Our accountant has found the tax forms.

Linking Verbs

"Stonewall is weary" is an example of a sentence with a **linking verb**. *Stonewall* is the subject and *is* is the linking verb. This verb does not describe action, because no action is happening. The *linking verb* is telling you something about Stonewall's condition. It links *Stonewall* and *weary*. You can use an equals sign to determine whether a verb is a linking verb. Stonewall = weary.

Following is a list of linking verbs. They are forms of the verb *to be: be, am, are, is, was, were, being, been.* Linking verbs are also verbs of the senses, such as *feel, look, hear, taste, smell, sound.* Other linking verbs include: *seem, remain, appear, become.*

As you have seen, these linking verbs are used also with active verbs to form verb phrases. When they are used strictly as linking verbs, they are non-action verbs. Rather, they link the subject and another word in the sentence that renames or describes the subject.

EXAMPLES

The cabin *feels* cozy.
   Cozy describes the cabin. *Feels* is the word that links *cabin* and *cozy.*

They *seem like* nice people.
   They and *people* are the same. The verb, *seem like,* links them.
   They and *people* equal each other.

Juan *is* a fan of MTV.
   Juan and *fan* are the same person. *Is* is the linking verb.

EXERCISE FOR PRACTICE

Underline the subject with one line and the linking verbs with <u>two lines</u> in the following sentences. When you complete the exercise, check the end of this section for the answers.

EXAMPLES

<u>You</u> <u>are</u> the winner!

<u>Batman</u> and <u>Robin</u> <u>remain</u> legends.

The <u>desk</u> <u>looks</u> old.

<u>Quimbe</u> <u>will be</u> captain.

1. That building was our research division.
2. The shipment appears to be your back order.
3. Lydia Ridgway has been our tax expert.
4. The pilots were skilled.
5. Apples taste good.
6. The proposal is our final draft.
7. The twins seem to be identical.
8. Rosebud feels sleepy.
9. The employees are new.
10. Casper will be a good salesman.

Passive Verbs

''The test was given by the instructor'' is an example of a sentence with a **passive verb**. *Test* is the subject, and *was given* is the passive verb phrase. When the verb is passive, the subject is being acted upon. In other words, when the verb is passive, the subject is *not* doing anything. It is not acting. (When the verb is active, the subject is acting.) The verb *was given* tells you what was done *to* the test. The subject, *test*, did not do anything; therefore the verb is passive.

EXAMPLES

The puppy *has been given* a bath.
Management *was asked* about the problem.
The program *will be checked* for coding errors.

Passive verbs are used when you don't want to draw attention to the one who is acting in the sentence (the subject). Passive verbs allow the one doing the acting to remain hidden. They draw attention to the action, and they focus on the one *receiving* the action. Because passive verbs are not as clear and direct as active verbs, use passive verbs sparingly. Only twenty percent of your sentences should use passive verbs.

When you use active and linking verbs in eighty percent of the sentences that you write, you will be writing in a clear style. Many people think that a clear style is too direct. They use passive verbs to avoid naming *who* is responsible. Sometimes they avoid naming the actor out of habit, or because their bosses or instructors write in a passive style. When they use passive verbs, they are avoiding responsibility, and they make the reader's job more difficult.

USE PASSIVE VERBS SPARINGLY!

EXERCISE FOR PRACTICE

In the following sentences, underline the subject with one line and the passive verb phrase (passive verbs always need helping verbs) with two lines. When you complete the exercise, check the end of this section for the answers.

EXAMPLES

A short paper was written about tall people.

The newspaper has been canceled.

You will be asked for a donation.

1. The memo was edited.
2. We have been given a difficult job.
3. Ellen will be promoted.
4. Three programmers should be assigned to the project.
5. Farquar might be allowed at the table.
6. My left sock has been lost in the washing machine.
7. The prince should have been kissed by the fair maiden.
8. The proposal was rejected by management.
9. A memo has been sent by the Guard Dog committee.
10. The task force will be notified.

Changing Passive Verbs to Active Verbs

If more than twenty percent of the verbs in your written documents are passive, begin now to change this habit. To change from passive verbs to active verbs, rewrite the sentence so that the *subject* is acting. In the following sentence, the subject is *not* acting, so the verb is passive:

The instructor was hired by the personnel director.

Instructor is the subject and *was hired* is the passive verb. To change the verb from passive to active, find the person in the sentence who did the hiring (the personnel director). *Personnel director* is the subject of the new sentence and the verb changes from passive to active.

The personnel director hired the instructor.

This sentence now has an active verb because the subject (personnel director) is doing the acting.

In sentences where the one performing the action is not mentioned, you may have to decide who the actor is. In other words, who is performing the action?

The memo was sent yesterday.

The sender of the memo is not named.
To write a sentence with an active verb, you must name the actor.

Lisa sent the memo yesterday.

Now the verb, *sent* is active. To change from writing passive verbs to writing active verbs, develop the habit of naming *who* or *what* did the acting. Sometimes you may not know who did the acting. In that case, change the verb from passive to active without changing the subject.

EXAMPLES

Passive: Students *were given* their grades.
Active: Students *received* their grades.

Passive: We *were notified* about the changes.
Active: We *heard* about the changes.

Passive: Our supervisor *has been awarded* a bonus by the Excellence Committee.
Active: The Excellence Committee *has awarded* a bonus to our supervisor.

Passive: A letter *was received* by Mr. Chan.
Active: Mr. Chan *received* a letter.

Passive: The dead trees *were removed* by the road crew.
Active: The road crew *removed* the dead trees.

Passive: The barn *has been rebuilt* by Farmer Jones.
Active: Farmer Jones *rebuilt* the barn.

Notice that the sentences with the active verbs are shorter. Short sentences are better than long sentences because they are easier to read. Always keep your sentences as short as possible. After twenty-two words in a sentence, a reader's attention drops rapidly.

EXERCISE FOR PRACTICE

In the following sentences, rewrite the sentence to change the passive verb or verb phrase into an active verb or verb phrase. The passive verbs and passive verb phrases are underlined. When you have completed the exercise check your answers at the end of this section.

EXAMPLES

Passive: The formula has been changed by the chemist.

Active: The chemist changed the formula.

Passive: Several books are recommended.

Active: The librarian recommended several books.

Passive: The audience was entertained by the comedian.

Active: The comedian entertained the audience.

1. Three computers were donated to the school by the programmers.

2. These guidelines have been changed by the director.

3. You were told by your dentist to brush your teeth after every meal.

4. Old clothing has been donated by our neighbors.

5. Headlines in the news are written too quickly.

6. He was overpaid, but he was worth it.

7. A wreath was laid on the tomb.

8. People's names can be remembered by using association.

9. A toast was offered by us to celebrate Jeremiah's birthday.

10. The students were given a vacation.

REVIEW EXERCISE FOR PRACTICE

To practice finding the three kinds of verbs we have studied, complete the following exercise. <u>Underline</u> the subject with one line and the verb or verb phrase with <u>two lines</u>. Identify the verbs as active (**A**) or passive (**P**) or linking (**L**) by placing the correct letter on the line next to the number. Before doing this exercise, you may want to review pages 10, 14 and 16, which define active, passive, and linking verbs. When you finish the exercise, check the end of this section for the answers.

EXAMPLES

_A_ The crystal <u>ball</u> <u>shattered</u>.

_P_ <u>We</u> <u>have been notified</u>.

_L_ Her <u>manager</u> <u>is</u> tall.

_____ **1.** They might go to the party.

_____ **2.** Dead leaves covered the deck.

_____ **3.** Those doctors are surgeons.

_____ **4.** The tests were taken during the lunch hour.

_____ **5.** Their shoes had been stolen.

_____ **6.** Six employees are leaving the building.

_____ **7.** The lake sparkled in the sun.

_____ **8.** I feel great!

_____ **9.** Two reports were submitted by the quality team.

_____ **10.** The vase is crystal.

COMPLETING THE SENTENCE CORE

Sentence cores must have subjects and verbs. Some sentence cores also have completers. **Completers** "complete" the idea expressed in the core. Sentences with active and linking verbs usually have completers, though not always. Sentences with passive verbs seldom have completers.

In this sentence, "Jake ordered shrimp," *Jake* is the subject, *ordered* is the verb, and *shrimp* is the completer. *Shrimp* tells what Jake ordered. It completes the idea expressed by the subject and the verb.

Some sentence cores do not have completers, because not all sentences need them. In this sentence, "The baby cried," a completer is not required because the idea is already complete. When a completer is present as part of the core, it will be a noun, a pronoun, or an adjective. In the examples below, the completer is shown in italics. Note that the completer follows the subject and verb and it does one of the following:

- **The completer renames the subject.**

  That ship is the *Queen Mary*.

  Ship and *Queen Mary* are the same thing. *Queen Mary* renames the word *ship*.

- **The completer tells who or what received the action of the active verb.**

  The architect changed the *design*.

  Design is the completer. The design is what the architect changed. *Design* receives the action of the active verb *changed*.

- **The completer describes the subject.**

  The book is *excellent*.

  Excellent is the completer. It describes the subject *book*.

EXERCISE FOR PRACTICE

In the following exercise, underline the subject with <u>one line</u>, the verb or verb phrase with <u>two lines</u>, and the completer in each sentence with a <u>broken line</u>. Beneath the sentence, circle the word that tells what the completer does. When you finish the exercise, check the end of this section for the answers.

EXAMPLES

<u>They</u> <u><u>are</u></u> late.

renames   receives   (describes)

<u>Mrs. Creampuff</u> <u><u>promoted</u></u> her secretary.

renames   (receives)   describes

The <u>writers</u> <u><u>were</u></u> Nobel Prize winners.

(renames)   receives   describes

1. The witches are restless.
    renames   receives   describes
2. The crowd booed the candidate.
    renames   receives   describes
3. Friday is the thirteenth.
    renames   receives   describes
4. Corpulo sounded upset.
    renames   receives   describes
5. We approved the contract.
    renames   receives   describes
6. The book that I am reading is *Gone with the Wind*.
    renames   receives   describes
7. Those four cars are Hondas.
    renames   receives   describes
8. Rambo completed the bicycle race.
    renames   receives   describes
9. Are you ticklish?
    renames   receives   describes
10. I accepted the job.
    renames   receives   describes

REVIEWING FOR RESULTS

EXERCISE FOR PRACTICE

The following exercise helps you identify the subjects, verbs, and completers used in sentences with CORE CONTROL. In each sentence below, <u>underline</u> the subject(s) with one line, the verb or verb phrase with <u>two lines</u> and the completer with a <u>broken line</u>. Remember that some sentences do not have completers. Identify the verbs as active (A) or passive (P) or linking (L) by placing the correct letter on the line next to the number. When you complete the exercise, check the end of this section for the correct answers.

EXAMPLES

_L_ The stockroom <u>door</u> <u>is</u> <u>stuck</u>.

_A_ <u>Harpo</u> <u>will announce</u> the retirement <u>plan</u>.

_P_ The <u>memo</u> <u>was sent</u> on Tuesday.

_____ **1.** Gary will order pizza.

_____ **2.** The salesman signed the order.

_____ **3.** She is tired.

_____ **4.** The doctor looked surprised.

_____ **5.** The Purchasing Department handles parts orders.

_____ **6.** Hal and Phil were chosen.

_____ **7.** Our manager quit.

_____ **8.** The doors have been painted.

_____ **9.** Tennis is a great sport.

_____ **10.** Tad signed the check.

_____ **11.** Rosie is absent.

_____ **12.** They left.

_____ **13.** I will be seeing her tomorrow.

_____ **14.** Two strangers appeared.

_____ **15.** The twins sang a duet.

EXERCISE FOR PRACTICE

This exercise reviews the principles of CORE CONTROL to be sure they are clear in your mind before we move to the next section. Choose words from the list below and fill in the blanks with the correct answers. Some words are used more than once. Check your answers at the end of this section.

_____ CONTROL is a formula to help you write clear _____.

A _____ is a group of words that make sense together. Every sentence has

a _____ and a _____. Some sentences have _____.

Use a _____ noun as a subject to help your reader see a _____ of

what you are saying. Use _____ verbs to show that the subject is acting.

Use _____ verbs to show the condition of the subject. _____ verbs

show that the subject is acted upon. _____ verbs should be used only for

variety or to focus on the act, rather than on the subject. When you use

_____ nouns, _____ or _____ verbs and a _____

(when one is present), you are using _____ CONTROL. You should use

this formula for _____ percent of your sentences in business writing.

completer	sentence(s)	subject
passive	linking	CORE
seed	active	picture
eighty	modifiers	incomplete
paragraph	twelve	verb

ANSWERS FOR SECTION I

Answers (page 4)

__I__ **1.** At our new offices on Main Street.

__I__ **2.** Really funny, but serious too.

__C__ **3.** Mr. Firbaugh's expense account is late again.

__I__ **4.** When I exercise, especially after work.

__C__ **5.** Tom stood there biting his nails.

__I__ **6.** But only when she wasn't looking.

__C__ **7.** Will I win if I buy a ticket?

__I__ **8.** Because he was boring!

__C__ **9.** Time flies.

__I__ **10.** For anyone who is concerned about money.

Answers (page 5)

1. She completed the test in ten minutes.

2. The Browns live next door.

3. Alice and Albert broke the lock on the old trunk.

4. The doors to the office were jammed.

5. Have you seen my manager?

6. Few forgive without a fuss.

7. We anchored the boat and jumped overboard to swim.

8. The billing went out yesterday.

9. They can't start the meeting without us.

10. Two fire engines raced through the parking lot.

Answers (page 8)

1. <u>Alfredo</u> is happy with the results.

2. Four <u>walls</u> fell during the earthquake.

3. The team <u>leader</u> won an award.

4. One (method) involves beating the bushes.

5. (Commitment) is important.

6. Two <u>bears</u> robbed our campsite.

7. Big (problems) faced the crew.

8. The right (answer) isn't always the best answer.

9. <u>Magicians</u> are a vanishing breed.

10. (Work) is about as much fun as you make it.

11. <u>Sinbad</u> parked on the lawn.

12. If at first you don't succeed, <u>you</u> are like the rest of us.

13. The lunch <u>room</u> is serving bean salad.

14. At midnight the <u>bells</u> chimed wildly.

15. The (blame) was traced to the computer.

Answers (page 9)

The seed nouns are underlined in the exercise below. Seed nouns are picture words—in other words, they are visual. They have substance and they occupy space.

1.	<u>Goldilocks</u>	7.	<u>programmer</u>
2.	for	8.	temper
3.	quality	9.	<u>we</u>
4.	<u>computer</u>	10.	<u>telephone</u>
5.	<u>guests</u>	11.	<u>clouds</u>
6.	gently	12.	jogging

Note: In number 12, the word *jogging* is an action. A *jogger* would be a seed noun.

Be sure that you have written four words that are seed nouns or pronouns. To check yourself, ask these questions: Are the words visual? Can I see them or touch them? Do they have substance? Do they occupy space? If your answer is yes, you have written four seed nouns or pronouns. These words are good subjects of sentences because you help your reader to "see" what you are saying. Remember, use seed nouns or pronouns in at least eighty percent of the sentences that you write. Here are four examples of seed nouns:

salad   *students*

you   *hospital*

Answers (page 11)

1. <u>Maryloubeth</u> <u>laughed</u> at the natives.

2. <u>Regis</u> <u>lives</u> in Toledo.

3. Our <u>manager</u> <u>believes</u> that quality is important.

4. Billbob's <u>team</u> <u>focuses</u> on teamwork.

5. The security <u>guard</u> <u>locked</u> the gate.

6. <u>She</u> <u>guards</u> his delicate secret.

7. A Japanese <u>guest</u> <u>toured</u> our office.

8. <u>They</u> <u>left</u>.

9. <u>Spotty</u> <u>barked</u> at the mail carrier.

10. The <u>concert</u> <u>ended</u>.

Answers (page 13)

1. <u>Birdie</u> <u>should receive</u> the award.

2. <u>Jeeves</u> <u>will show</u> you to the door.

3. <u>Mrs. Turtletaub</u> <u>has given</u> me another chance.

4. The training <u>director</u> <u>is announcing</u> the new class schedule.

5. Our <u>secretary</u> <u>will be routing</u> the memo through your office.

6. <u>We</u> <u>have told</u> him everything.

7. The <u>auditors</u> <u>will be completing</u> their work early.

8. The <u>furnace</u> <u>is behaving</u> strangely.

9. The <u>committee</u> <u>is giving</u> sweatshirts as prizes.

10. Our <u>accountant</u> <u>has found</u> the tax forms.

Answers (page 15)

1. That <u>building</u> <u><u>was</u></u> our research division.

2. The <u>shipment</u> <u><u>appears to be</u></u> your back order.

3. <u>Lydia Ridgway</u> <u><u>has been</u></u> our tax expert.

4. The <u>pilots</u> <u><u>were</u></u> skilled.

5. <u>Apples</u> <u><u>taste</u></u> good.

6. The <u>proposal</u> <u><u>is</u></u> our final draft.

7. The <u>twins</u> <u><u>seem to be</u></u> identical.

8. <u>Rosebud</u> <u><u>feels</u></u> sleepy.

9. The <u>employees</u> <u><u>are</u></u> new.

10. <u>Casper</u> <u><u>will be</u></u> a good salesman.

Answers (page 17)

1. The <u>memo</u> <u><u>was edited</u></u>.

2. <u>We</u> <u><u>have been given</u></u> a difficult job.

3. <u>Ellen</u> <u><u>will be promoted</u></u>.

4. Three <u>programmers</u> <u><u>should be assigned</u></u> to the project.

5. <u>Farquar</u> <u><u>might be allowed</u></u> at the table.

6. My left <u>sock</u> <u><u>has been lost</u></u> in the washing machine.

7. The <u>prince</u> <u><u>should have been kissed</u></u> by the fair maiden.

8. The <u>proposal</u> <u><u>was rejected</u></u> by management.

9. A <u>memo</u> <u><u>has been sent</u></u> by the Guard Dog committee.

10. The task <u>force</u> <u><u>will be notified</u></u>.

Answers (page 20)

1. Three computers <u>were donated</u> to the school by the programmers.

   The programmers <u>donated</u> three computers to the school.

2. These guidelines <u>have been changed</u> by the director.

   The director <u>changed</u> these guidelines.

3. You <u>were told</u> by your dentist to brush your teeth after every meal.

   Your dentist <u>told</u> you to brush your teeth after every meal.

4. Old clothing <u>has been donated</u> by our neighbors.

   Our neighbors <u>donated</u> old clothing.

5. Headlines in the news <u>are written</u> too quickly.

   Reporters <u>write</u> news headlines too quickly.

6. He <u>was overpaid</u>, but he was worth it.

   They <u>overpaid</u> him, but he was worth it.

7. A wreath <u>was laid</u> on the tomb.

   The mourners <u>laid</u> a wreath on the tomb.

8. People's names <u>can be remembered</u> by using association.

   You <u>can remember</u> people's names by using association.

9. A toast of champagne <u>was offered</u> by us to celebrate Jeremiah's birthday.

   We <u>offered</u> a champagne toast to celebrate Jeremiah's birthday.

   OR

   We <u>toasted</u> Jeremiah's birthday with champagne.

10. The students <u>were given</u> a vacation.

    The students <u>received</u> a vacation.

    OR

    The instructors <u>gave</u> the students a vacation.

32

Answers (page 21)

A   **1.** Those <u>might go</u> to the party.

A   **2.** Dead <u>leaves</u> <u>covered</u> the deck.

L   **3.** Those <u>doctors</u> <u>are</u> surgeons.

P   **4.** The <u>tests</u> <u>were taken</u> during the lunch hour.

P   **5.** Their <u>shoes</u> <u>had been stolen</u>.

A   **6.** Six <u>employees</u> <u>are leaving</u> the building.

A   **7.** The <u>lake</u> <u>sparkled</u> in the sun.

L   **8.** I <u>feel</u> great!

P   **9.** Two <u>reports</u> <u>were submitted</u> by the quality team.

L   **10.** The <u>vase</u> <u>is</u> crystal.

Answers (page 23)

1. The <u>witches</u> <u>are</u> restless.

    renames   receives   (describes)

2. The <u>crowd</u> <u>booed</u> the <u>candidate</u>.

    renames   (receives)   describes

3. <u>Friday</u> <u>is</u> the <u>thirteenth</u>.

    (renames)   receives   describes

4. <u>Corpulo</u> <u>sounded</u> <u>upset</u>.

    renames   receives   (describes)

5. <u>We</u> <u>approved</u> the <u>contract</u>.

    renames   (receives)   describes

6. The <u>book</u> that I am reading <u>is</u> *Gone with the Wind*.

    (renames)   receives   describes

7. Those four <u>cars</u> <u>are</u> <u>Hondas</u>.

    (renames)   receives   describes

8. <u>Rambo</u> <u>completed</u> the bicycle <u>race</u>.

    renames   (receives)   describes

9. <u>Are</u> <u>you</u> <u>ticklish</u>?

    renames   receives   (describes)

10. <u>I</u> <u>accepted</u> the <u>job</u>.

    renames   (receives)   describes

Answers (page 24)

A   1. Gary will order pizza.

A   2. The salesman signed the order.

L   3. She is tired.

L   4. The doctor looked surprised.

A   5. The Purchasing Department handles parts orders.

P   6. Hal and Phil were chosen.

A   7. Our manager quit.

P   8. The doors have been painted.

L   9. Tennis is a great sport.

A   10. Tad signed the check.

L   11. Rosie is absent.

A   12. They left.

A   13. I will be seeing her tomorrow.

A   14. Two strangers appeared.

A   15. The twins sang a duet.

Answers (page 25)

CORE CONTROL is a formula to help you write clear *sentences* . A *sentence* is a group of words that make sense together. Every sentence has a *subject* and a *verb* . Some sentences have *completers* . Use a *seed* noun as a subject to help your reader see a *picture* of what you are saying. Use *active* verbs to show that the subject is acting. Use *linking* verbs to show the condition of the subject. *Passive* verbs show that the subject is acted upon. *Passive* verbs should be used only for variety or to focus on the act, rather than on the subject. When you use *seed* nouns, *active* or *linking* verbs and a *completer* (when one is present), you are using *CORE* CONTROL. You should use this formula for *eighty* percent of your sentences in business writing.

SECTION 2

MODIFIERS

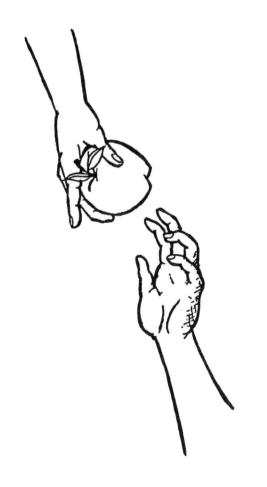

WHAT ARE MODIFIERS?

For our purposes, **modifiers** are *adjectives, adverbs* and *prepositional phrases* that give you more information about the sentence core.

EXAMPLE

Tex always wears red feathers in his hat.

The core is: *Tex* (subject), *wears* (verb), *feathers* (completer). The rest of the words are modifiers. *Always* is an adverb, *red* is an adjective; and *in his hat* is a prepositional phrase. Each modifier is explained in more detail in this section of the book.

Modifiers always appear in relation to some other word. They describe or limit the words they are modifying. They are a part of almost all sentences. They give you more information about the core, and they make the meaning of the core clear and exact. Modifiers make the core more ''a-peeling.''

EXAMPLE

Mrs. Beebrow left her office.

The core is: *Mrs. Beebrow* (subject); *left* (verb); *office* (completer). By adding modifiers (adjectives, adverbs, and prepositional phrases), you will have a clearer and more exact picture of Mrs. Beebrow. You will know when she left the office, what kind of person she is, how she left, what size her office is, and where her office is.

EXAMPLE

(At three o'clock) (gentle) Mrs. Beebrow *(quietly)* left
(her) (small) office *(on the second floor)*.

Each of the words or phrases in italics is a modifier. Let's look at each kind of modifier in more detail.

EASY ADJECTIVES

Adjectives are easy. They are single words that always modify (describe), qualify, or limit a noun or pronoun. In English, an adjective appears in front of the noun or pronoun that it is describing.

EXAMPLE

Wolfgang tickled her curly toes.

Her and *curly* are adjectives describing the noun toes. The adjectives in the examples below are in italics:

EXAMPLES

hot pizza   *miserly* manager
strict policy   *Dear* John
extra candy   *happy* camper
profound professor   *welcome* paycheck

EXERCISE FOR PRACTICE

In the following exercise, put (parentheses) around the adjectives and <u>underline</u> the seed noun that is modified. Check the end of this section for the answers.

EXAMPLES

(creative) <u>designer</u>
(helpful) <u>employee</u>
(two) (small) <u>cupcakes</u>
(empty) <u>drawers</u>

1. wild strawberries
2. old letters
3. corporate office
4. wrinkled suit
5. sweet old grandmother

6. funny money
7. final report
8. red and green lights
9. curious tourists
10. smart student

EXERCISE FOR PRACTICE

In the following longer phrases, which also include other kinds of modifiers (*adverbs* and *prepositional phrases*), place (parentheses) around the adjectives and underline the seed nouns that they modify. Note that the groups of words in this exercise are *not* complete sentences. When you have finished, check the end of this section for the correct answers.

EXAMPLES

(three) (math) <u>classes</u> in (four) <u>years</u>

(new) (exercise) <u>machines</u> for the (athletic) <u>club</u>

a (few) (kind) <u>words</u> and (polite) <u>applause</u>

1. three important visitors from the home office

2. the old carpet in the new kitchen

3. IBM computers and additional hardware

4. software engineers at the computer conference

5. furry creatures from the black lagoon

6. the sleeping guard at the south gate

7. a lemon pie and a chocolate cake on the card table

8. several colorful new stamps from the Post Office

9. a serious complaint letter to the manager about her outrageous bill

THE PREPOSITIONAL PHRASE MAZE

A **prepositional phrase** is also a modifier. It is a group of words that follows the noun or pronoun that it is modifying. For example, in the phrase "flowers in the vase," *flowers* is a noun and *in the vase* is a prepositional phrase that modifies *flowers.*

A prepositional phrase gives you more information about a noun. A prepositional phrase consists of a preposition and an object. The preposition itself is a connecting word; it connects the noun or pronoun that follows it (the object of the preposition) with some other word in the sentence.

EXAMPLE

The sunburn on her back was bright red.

On her back is a prepositional phrase. The preposition is the word *on. On* connects the word *sunburn* to the word *back. On* tells where the sunburn is.

In the phrase "trees in the forest," *trees* is a noun. *In the forest* is a prepositional phrase modifying the noun *trees. In* is the preposition (the word that connects *trees* and *forest). In* tells you where the trees are in relation to the forest. *Forest* is the **object of the preposition**. It tells you what the trees are in.

To help you remember what prepositions are, think of a squirrel and a stump. Any way that a squirrel can relate to a stump is a **preposition**.

The squirrel is *in* the stump.
The squirrel is *on* the stump.
The squirrel is not happy *despite* the stump.
The squirrel will not be happy *until* the stump is gone.
News *concerning* the stump reached the squirrel.
The squirrel moved *toward* the stump.

Two lists of prepositions follow. One is a list of **simple prepositions**, or single-word prepositions. The second list is **group prepositions**, or prepositions of more than one word.

COMMONLY USED PREPOSITIONS

Simple Prepositions

about	by	onto
above	concerning	out
across	despite	out of
after	down	outside
against	due to	since
along	during	through
among	for	throughout
around	from	to
as	in	toward
at	inside	under
before	into	underneath
below	like	until
beneath	near(by)	up
beside(s)	of	with
between	off	within
beyond	on	without

Group Prepositions

according to	by way of	in place of
along with	in addition to	in spite of
as well as	in back of	instead of
because of	in conjunction with	on account of
by means of	in front of	outside of

Ending Sentences with Prepositions

In the past, it was considered improper to end a sentence with a preposition. Today, however, you can end sentences with anything you choose (almost), including prepositions. English is less formal now, and everyday speech patterns and sentence rhythms allow sentences to end with prepositions. Some sentences sound silly when we force outdated preposition rules on them.

Examples of Ending Sentences with Prepositions

No: What is it *for* which you are looking?
Yes: What are you looking *for*?

No: Wally had no one to whom *to* turn.
Yes: Wally had no one to turn *to.*

No: They had many exciting adventures *about* which to talk.
Yes: They had many exciting adventures to talk *about.*

Winston Churchill and Prepositions

Winston Churchill was famous for his use of proper English. Once he sent a report to his secretary of state for proofreading. The secretary sent back a note with the report that stated, "Sir Winston, you have ended a sentence with a preposition." Sir Winston shot back a sharp reply that read, "Absurd! This is the kind of silly writing up with which I will not put!"

Peculiar Prepositions (Idioms)

All languages have idioms—the peculiar expressions that come from daily use by many people over time. Idioms do not always fit the strict rules of grammar. They are often formed by a combination of prepositions and certain verbs, nouns, and adjectives. Listed below are common idioms that are formed by adding prepositions to other parts of speech. The dictionary tells you whether an expression is an idiom.

	Prepositional Idioms	(read across)
abstain from	acquit of	addicted to
adept in	adhere to	agree to (a thing)
agree with (a person)	angry at (a thing)	angry with (a person)
averse to	capable of	characteristic of
compare to (for an example)	compare with (to illustrate a point)	
concern in	concerned with	desire for
desirous of	devoid of	differ about
differ from (things)	differ with (a person)	different from
disagree with	disdain for	disdain for
envious of	empty of	expert in
foreign to	hint at	identical with
independent of	infer from	inseparable from
jealous of	oblivious of	prerequisite to
prior to	proficient in	profit by
prohibit from	protect against	reason with
regret for	repugnant to	sensitive to
separate from	substitute for	superior to
sympathize with	tamper with	unmindful of

EXERCISE FOR PRACTICE

In the following exercise, put (parentheses) around the prepositional phrases in each sentence. Note that some prepositional phrases include adjectives within the phrase:

EXAMPLE

candy with a dark chocolate center

Candy is the noun that is modified by the prepositional phrase. *With a dark chocolate center* is the complete prepositional phrase (*with* is the preposition and *center* is the object of the preposition). *Dark* and *chocolate* are **adjectives** modifying *center*. In this exercise, put (parentheses) around only the prepositional phrases. When you are finished, check the end of the section for the answers.

EXAMPLES

Old Klondike sat (on the ice) (in the cold Arctic snow).
Put the new equipment (on the counter) (near the window).
(In two weeks) we will have visitors (from Southwest Africa).

1. The enrollment forms for the class are in the files under the desk.
2. Pedro went to the branch office in Utah.
3. Hans wrote to the instructor of the class in public speaking.
4. Everyone on the committee is welcome to my opinion.
5. We wouldn't leave without you.
6. Waldo sat in front of us at the movies.
7. We have set the meeting for next Wednesday in my office.
8. In one week, the stone building on the north corner sold for two million dollars.
9. On the map, we saw a road through the pass to the old gold mine.
10. I have given up my search for truth and I am looking for a good fantasy.

EXERCISE FOR PRACTICE

In the following sentences, add, change, or delete prepositions to make the sentence clear. Check the end of this section for answers when you are finished.

EXAMPLES

Add *up* the bill.

Hallie read the text ~~about~~ (economics) eagerly.

The princess didn't know (for) what to ask.

Your answers are different *from* ~~than~~ mine.

1. They finished up their meeting.

2. Giles left prior of our meeting.

3. The figures of the audit are ready for you in the office of the vice president.

4. JohnBoy felt superior of his friend.

5. Alonzo is a hard person with whom to deal.

6. Let's go over to the factory this afternoon.

7. Sylvia has no regret of her choice.

8. Gertie wrote the report about the earnings of the company for the manager of finance.

9. Warren's disdain of the system is complete.

10. Let's sit down in the conference room.

EXERCISE FOR PRACTICE

Complete the following sentences with the correct idioms. Check your answers at the end of this section when you are finished.

EXAMPLES

Agree _with_ me now and save time later.
Why are you concerned _with_ this project?
Eggs are a substitute _for_ meat.

1. I can't agree _____ your terms.

2. What are you hinting _____?

3. Millie's desire _____ chocolate overcame her strong resolve.

4. We hope to profit _____ the investment.

5. When I say "yes," please try to reason _____ me.

6. This meteor is different _____ that one.

7. Travel is foreign _____ me.

8. I have no regret _____ my decision.

9. I infer _____ your statement that you have no solution, but you greatly admire the problem.

10. I am envious _____ your ability to sit here until life gets easier.

BLURBS ABOUT ADVERBS

Adverbs are single words that often modify the verb in a sentence.

EXAMPLE

He knocked sharply.

Sharply is the adverb and it tells *how* he knocked. Adverbs answer the question how, when, and why. Adverbs also modify adjectives and other adverbs.

EXAMPLE

Violet has a reasonably secure future.

Reasonably modifies *secure*, which is an adjective.

EXAMPLE

She loved him most dearly.
   Most is an adverb modifying *dearly*, which is also an adverb.

Many adverbs end in *-ly*. . .but not all of them! Below is a list of adverbs that do *not* end in *-ly*. Become familiar with them and avoid the "adverb blues."

almost	around	down	here	now
often	quite	soon	still	then
too	very	when	yet	just

EXERCISE FOR PRACTICE

Place (parentheses) around the adverbs in the following sentences. One sentence has two adverbs. Check your answers at the end of this section when you are finished.

EXAMPLES

They are (very) (happily) married.
Very is an adverb modifying *happily*, which is also an adverb.

I'll be (quite) unhappy if you keep trying to improve things.
The adverb *quite* modifies the adjective *unhappy*.

Mork explained the letter (quite) (carefully).
Quite is an adverb modifying *carefully*, which is also an adverb.
Carefully modifies the verb *explained*.

48

1. The pig turned slowly over the flames.

2. That report is badly written.

3. Cassandra was too nervous to go.

4. Please rescue me soon.

5. If you can survive death, you can probably survive anything.

6. Hiram almost won the Elvis Lookalike contest.

7. We simply will not wait.

8. You can more easily understand me if you read my lips.

9. Natural gas is certainly a better choice for clean heating.

10. We took her fleeting pulse hourly.

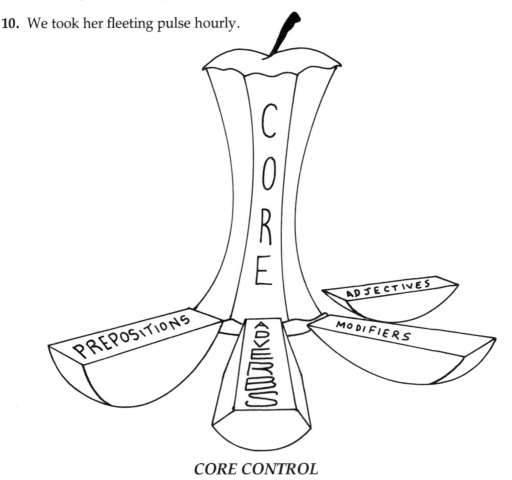

CORE CONTROL

REVIEWING FOR RESULTS

The following exercises will help you remember CORE CONTROL and how to use modifiers. You are now working with complete sentences, identifying the cores and modifiers, to see how they work together to create a complete picture for your reader. Sentence cores, especially verbs, are emphasized in these exercises because you will have the most control of your writing when you know how to find—and how to control—the core. In addition, your readers will thank you for making their jobs easier.

EXERCISE FOR PRACTICE

In the following sentences, find the words that make up the sentence core. Underline the subject(s) with <u>one line</u>, the verb or verb phrase with <u>two lines</u>, and the completer with a <u>broken line</u>, if a completer is present. Note that all verbs in this exercise are active verbs. When you are finished, check your answers at the end of this section.

EXAMPLES

<u>We</u> <u>found</u> the <u>key</u> under the mat.

<u>Biff</u> and <u>Bart</u> <u>begged</u> the <u>baker</u> for banana bread.

<u>They</u> <u>will be leaving</u> the parking <u>lot</u> at 7:00 a.m.

1. We made lemonade for the picnic.
2. On Tuesday, the auditor filed his quarterly report.
3. Matilda wrote an angry letter to the collection agency.
4. Our department has acquired two new paper pushers.
5. The managers and the teams have been working on a difficult project.

50

EXERCISE FOR PRACTICE

In the following sentences, find the words that make up the sentence core. Underline the subject with <u>one line</u>, the verb or verb phrase with <u>two lines</u> and the completer with a <u>broken line</u>. Note that all verbs in this exercise are linking verbs. Check the answers at the end of this section when you are finished.

EXAMPLES

The <u>zookeeper</u> <u>seems</u> <u>upset.</u>

<u>Charles</u> <u>will be</u> <u>King of England.</u>

Thor's aftershave <u>lotion</u> <u>smells</u> <u>wonderful.</u>

1. These policies are insane.
2. The retired couples were happy with their new freedom.
3. Monday will be a holiday at the bank.
4. Their cottage feels cozy.
5. *E.T.* is still a great movie.

EXERCISE FOR PRACTICE

In the following sentences, find the words that make up the sentence core. Underline the subject(s) with <u>one line</u> and the passive verb phrase with <u>two lines</u>.

Most passive verbs do not have completers. Note that all verbs in this exercise are passive verbs. Passive verbs should be used in only twenty percent of your sentences. They are not usually good choices, because they often make a sentence longer than it needs to be. Passive verbs are also harder to process mentally because they do not focus on the subject. This exercise helps you recognize passive verbs so that you can control your use of them.

EXAMPLES

The <u>system</u> <u>can be disrupted</u> totally if we all work together.

After lunch, <u>Lucy</u> <u>was presented</u> with the Best Posture Award.

While waiting for the bus, <u>Herkimer</u> <u>was struck</u> by an outrageous idea.

1. Phillip has been known to eat broccoli.
2. A complete review was given to their request for funds.
3. The troops were informed that communication had completely broken down.
4. The proposal was written in three sections.
5. Scientists have not been educated as writers.

EXERCISE FOR PRACTICE

In the following sentences, find the words that make up the sentence core. Underline the subject with <u>one line</u>, the verb phrase with <u>two lines</u>, and the completer, if one is present, with a <u>broken line</u>. Next, put (parentheses) around all of the modifiers. The names of the modifiers are identified for you on the answer page: (adj) adjective, (adv) adverb, or (p.p.) prepositional phrase. Check the end of this section for the answers. (Do not bother to identify the word *the*. It is called an **article**, along with the words *a* and *and*. Articles appear before nouns or adjectives.)

EXAMPLES

(My) mind is open, (by appointment) (only.)

(Our) (alert) staff discovered a major error (in the final figures.)

(My) (young) assistant was awarded a trip (to Hawaii.)

1. The connecting cable fits easily under the false floor.
2. Our quality expert presented to our staff the most up-to-date methods of quality control.
3. Men have become the tools of their tools.—*Henry David Thoreau*
4. Single-handedly, I have fought my way into this hopeless mess.
5. Two strong ropes held the climbers on the dangerous ledge.
6. Several students from Taiwan won the achievement awards.
7. His report extensively outlined NASA's future space plans for the lunar project.
8. George was liked by a small, select group of confused people.
9. On Tuesday we reviewed the brochure from the real estate agent in Seattle.
10. The new machinery was accidentally delivered to the wrong address.

Answers (page 38)

1. (wild) strawberries
2. (old) letters
3. (corporate) office
4. (wrinkled) suit
5. (sweet) (old) grandmother

6. (funny) money
7. (final) report
8. (red) and (green) lights
9. (curious) tourists
10. (smart) student

Answers (page 39)

1. (three) (important) visitors from the (home) office
2. the (old) carpet in the (new) kitchen
3. (IBM) computers and (additional) hardware
4. (software) engineers at the (computer) conference
5. (furry) creatures from the (black) lagoon
6. the (sleeping) guard at the (south) gate
7. a (lemon) pie and a (chocolate) cake on the (card) table
8. (several) (colorful) (new) stamps from the Post Office
9. a (serious) (complaint) letter to the manager about (her) (outrageous) bill

Answers (page 44)

1. The enrollment forms (for the class) are (in the files) (under the desk.)
2. Pedro went (to the branch office) (in Utah.)
3. Hans wrote (to the instructor) (of the class) (in public speaking.)
4. Everyone (on the committee) is welcome (to my opinion.)
5. We wouldn't leave (without you.)
6. Waldo sat (in front) (of us) (at the movies.)
7. We have set the meeting (for next Wednesday) (in my office.)
8. (In one week,) the stone building (on the north corner) sold (for two million dollars.)
9. (On the map,) we saw a road (through the pass) (to the old gold mine.)
10. I have given up my search (for truth) and I am looking (for a good fantasy.)

Answers (page 45)

1. They finished their meeting.

2. Giles left prior to our meeting.

3. The audit figures are ready for you in the vice president's office.

4. JohnBoy felt superior to his friend.

5. Alonzo is a hard person to deal with.

6. Let's go to the factory this afternoon.

7. Sylvia has no regret for her choice.

8. Gertie wrote the company earnings report for the finance manager.

9. Warren's disdain for the system is complete.

10. Let's sit in the conference room.

Answers (page 46)

1. I can't agree _to_ your terms.

2. What are you hinting _at_?

3. Millie's desire _for_ chocolate overcame her strong resolve.

4. We hope to profit _by_ the investment.

5. When I say "yes," please try to reason _with_ me.

6. This meteor is different _from_ that one.

7. Travel is foreign _to_ me.

8. I have no regret _for_ my decision.

9. I infer _from_ your statement that you have no solution, but you greatly admire the problem.

10. I am envious _of_ your ability to sit here until life gets easier.

Answers (page 48)

1. The pig turned (slowly) over the flames.
2. That report is (badly) written.
3. Cassandra was (too) nervous to go.
4. Please rescue me (soon).
5. If you can survive death, you can (probably) survive anything.
6. Hiram (almost) won the Elvis Lookalike contest.
7. We (simply) will (not) wait.
8. You can more (easily) understand me if you read my lips.
9. Natural gas is (certainly) a better choice for clean heating.
10. We took her fleeting pulse (hourly.)

Answers (page 49)

1. We made lemonade for the picnic.
2. On Tuesday, the auditor filed his quarterly report.
3. Matilda wrote an angry letter to the collection agency.
4. Our department has acquired two new paper pushers.
5. The managers and the teams have been working on a difficult project.

Answers (page 50)

1. These policies are insane.
2. The retired couples were happy with their new freedom.
3. Monday will be a holiday at the bank.
4. Their cottage feels cozy.
5. E.T. is still a great movie.

Answers (page 50)

1. <u>Phillip</u> <u>has been known</u> to eat broccoli.

2. A complete <u>review</u> <u>was given</u> to their request for funds.

3. The <u>troops</u> <u>were informed</u> that communication had completely broken down.

4. The <u>proposal</u> <u>was written</u> in three sections.

5. <u>Scientists</u> <u>have</u> not <u>been educated</u> as writers.

Answers (page 51)

1. The (connecting) [*adj.*] <u>cable</u> <u>fits</u> (easily) [*adv.*] (under the false floor.) [*p.p.*]

2. (Our) [*adj.*] (quality) [*adj.*] <u>expert</u> <u>presented</u> (to our staff) [*p.p.*] the (most) [*adv.*] (up-to-date) [*adj.*] <u>methods</u> (of quality control.) [*p.p.*]

3. <u>Men</u> <u>have become</u> the <u>tools</u> (of their tools.) [*p.p.*]—*Henry David Thoreau.*

4. (Single-handedly,) [*adv.*] <u>I</u> <u>have fought</u> (my) [*adj.*] <u>way</u> (into this hopeless mess.) [*p.p.*]

5. (Two) [*adj.*] (strong) [*adj.*] <u>ropes</u> <u>held</u> the <u>climbers</u> (on the dangerous ledge.) [*p.p.*]

6. (Several) [*adj.*] <u>students</u> (from Taiwan) [*p.p.*] <u>won</u> the (achievement) [*adj.*] <u>awards.</u>

7. (His) [*adj.*] <u>report</u> (extensively) [*adv.*] <u>outlined</u> (NASA's) [*adj.*] (future) [*adj.*] (space) [*adj.*] <u>plans</u> (for the lunar project.) [*p.p.*]

8. <u>George</u> <u>was liked</u> (by a small, select group) [*p.p.*] (of confused people.) [*p.p.*]

9. (On Tuesday) [*p.p.*] <u>we</u> <u>reviewed</u> the <u>brochure</u> (from the real estate agent) [*p.p.*] (in Seattle.) [*p.p.*]

10. The (new) [*adj.*] <u>machinery</u> <u>was</u> (accidentally) [*adv.*] <u>delivered</u> (to the wrong address.) [*p.p.*]

SECTION 3

SIGNAL WORDS

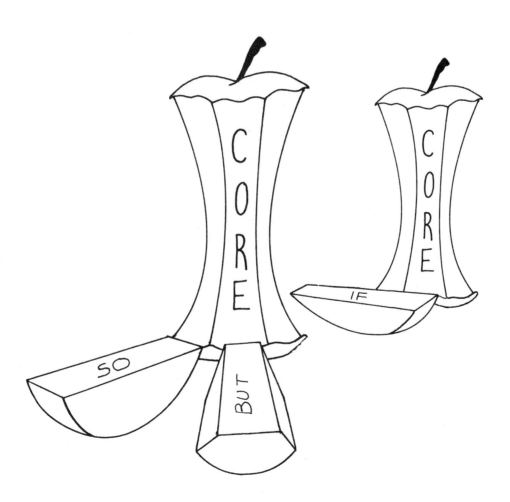

WHAT ARE SIGNAL WORDS?

Signal words are connecting words that help you create longer sentences. Until now, you have been writing simple sentences with only one core. Many sentences have two or more cores. Some cores are independent and can stand alone, while others are dependent and do not make sense by themselves. Signal words are the connecting words that make several cores possible in one sentence.

EXAMPLE

I can do without the basics, but I must have my luxuries.

This example has two cores. *I can do without the basics* is one core. *I must have my luxuries* is another core. The signal word that connects the two cores is the word *but*. The two cores, joined by the signal word *but*, are called a **compound sentence.**

In this section we are using two kinds of signal words. First, we are using signal words that introduce dependent cores. In your eighth-grade grammar book they were called **dependent clauses**.

EXAMPLE

If I leave now, I can attend the class.

If I leave now is the dependent core. It is dependent because it cannot stand alone as a sentence. *If* is the signal word that introduces the dependent core. This core is dependent on the independent core, *I can still attend the class.*

We also use signal words to join independent cores (also called **independent clauses**).

EXAMPLE

The bus was late so I missed the meeting.

So is the signal word that joins the two independent cores.

Signal words help you write sentences with more than one core. Use several cores when you want to write longer sentences or express more complex ideas. You can also explain cause and effect. Finally, you can use more than one core to connect ideas that are closely related.

EXAMPLE

The snow fell harder and the road closed ahead of us.

Your readers may not notice that you are using more than one core, but they *will* notice that your writing has plenty of variety, it is interesting, ideas are well connected, and your writing is easy to read.

A PAUSE FOR THE CLAUSE

In English grammar, cores are called **clauses**. If you are more familiar with the term *clause*, feel free to use that term instead of *core*. Cores, or clauses, are simple sentences that are used as parts of longer sentences. Some cores (clauses) are dependent and some are independent. A core is **dependent** when it has a subject and a verb, but it cannot stand alone as a sentence.

EXAMPLE

If you like our work, please refer us to others.

If you like our work is a dependent core, because it cannot stand alone as a complete sentence. *If you like our work* is dependent upon the rest of the sentence for its meaning. The remainder of the sentence, *please refer us to others*, is an independent core (clause) because it can stand alone as a complete sentence. Thus, *If you like our work, please refer us to others* has one dependent core and one independent core.

A Dependent Core...and One More

The following list contains words that introduce dependent cores. If any of the words on this list introduce a core, that core will be dependent—it cannot stand alone as a complete sentence.

Signal Words That Introduce Dependent Cores			
after	except	then	whether
although	if	though	which
as	since	unless	who
because	so that	when	whom
before	than	where	whose
even, even though	that	wherever	

EXAMPLE

After we met the prince, we went to lunch.

After we met the prince is a dependent core. The word that makes the core dependent is *after*. *After* is the signal word that introduces the dependent core. *We went to lunch* is the independent core. It can stand alone as a complete sentence. The dependent core must connect to the independent core, because a dependent core cannot stand alone. In the example above, the dependent core comes *before* the independent core.

EXAMPLE

The finance charges were so high that we decided to pay cash.

That we decided to pay cash is a dependent core, introduced by the signal word *that*. *That* is the word we use most often to make a core dependent. The first core, *The finance charges were so high*, is the independent core. The dependent core *that we decided to pay cash* depends on the independent core for its meaning. Notice that in this sentence the dependent core comes *after* the independent core. As a writer, you can choose whether you want the dependent core to come before or after the independent core.

Complex Sentences, a Simple Sentence...Plus

When a sentence has one independent core and one (or more) dependent cores, it is called a **complex sentence**. Complex does not mean difficult. It means that the sentence has one independent core plus at least one dependent core.

EXERCISE FOR PRACTICE

In the following sentences, circle the signal word that introduces the dependent core and underline the dependent core. When you have finished, check the end of this section for the answers.

EXAMPLES

They called their attorney (because) the agreement was not signed.

(As) the deadline approached, we put the report together quickly.

Most people become more interesting (when) they stop talking.

1. Get the facts first, then you can distort them as you please.—*Mark Twain*

2. Since we don't have anything else to do, let's bicker.

3. Pauli heard that the interview was canceled.

4. Because the circuit contains logic, the channel shifts by itself.

5. The mechanics needed more parts, which the suppliers provided.

6. If you write short sentences, your readers will like you better.

7. Let's go, before they ask us to do something.

8. When you are right, you are harder to forgive.

9. I would have an empty life if I had nothing to regret.

10. We thought that you would buy the tickets for us.

COMPOUND SENTENCES: TWO INDEPENDENT CORES, SOMETIMES MORE...

When a sentence has two independent cores (clauses) joined by a signal word that coordinates them, it is called a **compound sentence**. Both cores in the compound sentence make sense by themselves, and they could stand alone. However, the two cores express closely related ideas, so they are often joined to form one sentence. The following list contains signal words that are used to join two independent cores.

Signal Words That Join Independent Cores	
and	neither
but	nor
consequently	or
either	so
for	therefore
however	whereas
moreover	yet
namely	

EXAMPLES

The snow was deep, so I was late.
> *So* is the word that joins the two independent cores.

The food here is terrible and the portions are small.—*Woody Allen*
> *And* is the word that joins the two independent cores.

EXERCISE FOR PRACTICE

(Circle) the signal word that joins the two independent cores. Check your answers at the end of this section when you are finished.

EXAMPLES

The Materials Department makes structural studies, (and) the engineers write the specifications.

The text developed in a clear, logical order; (however) it did not have enough examples.

1. I had a wonderful idea last night, but I didn't like it.

2. We're planning a trip, so I bought traveler's checks.

3. The meeting was scheduled for 8:00; however, it began at 7:30.

4. I have just discovered the truth, and I can't understand why everyone isn't eager to hear it.

5. We do not give enough verbal feedback, nor do we get it.

6. The team cannot find the data; therefore, they are giving up the search.

7. Funny people are everywhere, and not all of them belong to the Army.

8. I can't remember what battle I'm fighting; moreover, I can't remember which side I'm on.

9. I'll go with you, or you can go with me.

10. The land deeds were lost for years, yet they continued to search.

REVIEWING FOR RESULTS

The following chart reviews possible core combinations you can use to create different sentence cores. Use compound and complex sentences for variety, and for expressing more complex ideas that are closely related.

Combining Sentence Cores

Type of Sentence	Number and Type of Core	Example
Simple sentence	One independent core	I wrote the letter.
Compound sentence	Two independent cores	I wrote the letter and he edited it.
Complex sentence	One independent core and one or more dependent cores	When I wrote the letter, he edited it.
Compound-complex sentence	Two independent cores and one or more dependent cores	When the manager requested the data I wrote the letter and he edited it.

66

EXERCISE FOR PRACTICE

In the following sentences, identify each sentence as simple (**S**), compound (**CD**), or complex (**CX**). Use the charts on pages 60 and 63 to help you. Check your answers at the end of this section when you are finished.

EXAMPLES

__S__ Most people mistake motion for action.

__CD__ A staff assistant is writing the report and the vice president will sign it.

__CX__ Unless we cut costs, we will go bankrupt.

1. _____ Abe reviewed the budget.

2. _____ A good English sentence is short, simple, and clear.

3. _____ Until I hear from you, I'll leave the light on.

4. _____ All employees are encouraged to contribute to the Family Relief Fund.

5. _____ You couldn't get me on Mars if it were the last place on earth.—*Erma Bombeck*

6. _____ He wanted my opinion and he gave it to me.

7. _____ We need some new clichés.

8. _____ My résumé, which I wrote last month, is on your desk.

9. _____ We wish to increase our business, so we are sending you a sample of our new product.

10. _____ I don't need the world, but I like to know it's still there.

Answers (page 62)

1. Get the facts first, (then) you can distort them as you please. —*Mark Twain*
2. (Since) we don't have anything else to do, let's bicker.
3. Pauli heard (that) the interview was canceled.
4. (Because) the circuit contains logic, the channel shifts by itself.
5. The mechanics needed more parts, (which) the suppliers provided.
6. (If) you write short sentences, your readers will like you better.
7. Let's go, (before) they ask us to do something.
8. (When) you are right, you are harder to forgive.
9. I would have an empty life (if) I had nothing to regret.
10. We thought (that) you would buy the tickets for us.

Answers (page 64)

1. I had a wonderful idea last night, (but) I didn't like it.
2. We're planning a trip, (so) I bought traveler's checks.
3. The meeting was scheduled for 8:00; (however), it began at 7:30.
4. I have just discovered the truth, (and) I can't understand why everyone isn't eager to hear it.
5. We do not give enough verbal feedback, (nor) do we get it.
6. The team cannot find the data; (therefore), they are giving up the search.
7. Funny people are everywhere, (and) not all of them belong to the Army.
8. I can't remember what battle I'm fighting; (moreover), I can't remember which side I'm on.
9. I'll go with you, (or) you can go with me.
10. The land deeds were lost for years, (yet) they continued to search.

Answers (page 66)

1. __S__ Abe reviewed the budget.

2. __S__ A good English sentence is short, simple, and clear.

3. __CX__ Until I hear from you, I'll leave the light on.

4. __S__ All employees are encouraged to contribute to the Family Relief Fund.

5. __CX__ You couldn't get me on Mars if it were the last place on earth.—*Erma Bombeck*

6. __CD__ He wanted my opinion and he gave it to me.

7. __S__ We need some new clichés.

8. __CX__ My résumé, which I wrote last month, is on your desk.

9. __CD__ We wish to increase our business, so we are sending you a sample of our new product.

10. __CD__ I don't need the world, but I like to know it's still there.

If you were able to complete this exercise easily, you are on your way to using CORE CONTROL successfully. Congratulations! To maintain your new skills, write practice sentences of your own using CORE CONTROL. Practice writing simple, compound, and complex sentences. When you write letters and memos, use these different kinds of sentences to add variety to your writing. You will keep your readers' interest, and you will expand the number of choices you have for expressing your ideas.

SECTION 4

PURPOSEFUL PARAGRAPHS

WHAT IS A PARAGRAPH?

A paragraph is a group of related sentences about one topic or idea. Each sentence fits into a logical pattern and relates to the other sentences in the paragraph. A well-written paragraph is like a bushel of tasty apples. The main idea of the paragraph is called the **topic sentence**. It is usually the first sentence in a paragraph. The topic sentence is the basket that holds the sentences (apples) together. The sentences that follow the topic sentence develop the topic sentence in a clear, orderly arrangement of supporting details. Sentences in a paragraph should have a close connection to the topic sentence. Sentences in the paragraph that do not relate to the topic sentence should be left out.

Paragraphs vary in length. Most are two to eight sentences; however, some paragraphs are only one sentence. One-sentence paragraphs do not give you the chance to develop your ideas, so they should not be used too often.

Using CORE CONTROL to Write Paragraphs

We can apply CORE CONTROL to paragraphs as well as to sentences. CORE CONTROL is achieved by using seed nouns as subjects in every sentence within the paragraph. All the sentence subjects should relate to each other in some way. In the following paragraph, the subject of each sentence is circled. Notice how the subjects of the sentences are all the same person, with one exception. The exception provides variety, so that the CORE CONTROL is not too rigid. One method of maintaining CORE CONTROL in paragraphs is by making the subject of each sentence the same. Remember to use seed nouns as subjects.

EXAMPLE

1. Perhaps Quarterback Hashbacker should retire from football. In the last game, he completed only four out of eighteen passes, and three were intercepted. Also he was dropped twice for a loss when the defensive line charged through. Although a recent heel injury might account for a pickup of only eighteen yards rushing he shouldn't be excused for the crucial fumbles. In the end, the team won by two points: a safety. Hashbacker wasn't on the field to take credit for the victory.

The subjects of sentences in paragraphs do not have to be the same word each time in order to have CORE CONTROL. You can also use subjects in the same category so that they are all about the same topic or idea. In the following paragraph, the subject of each sentence is circled. Notice that each subject is a seed noun, and that each subject relates to the others.

EXAMPLE

2. Visible products are easier to sell than services that you cannot see. For example, cars are easier to sell than consulting services. Buyers of products can judge the value and usefulness of a product quickly and easily by looking at it and by testing it. On the other hand, sellers of services must build trusting relationships with the buyer. They must prove that the buyer is getting good results, that the quality of the service will remain high, and that the pricing is fair. Businesses that sell services are really selling themselves. Customers demand quality in both products and services, but those who sell services face the most difficult challenge. Thus, people who are focused on customer relations have the best chance of succeeding in service-based businesses.

Some paragraphs do not have stated subjects. These paragraphs begin with active verbs and consist of a series of polite commands. The subject of each sentence is understood to be the word *you* as in "You press the key." These sentences are used most often to give instructions or to make polite requests. You are using CORE CONTROL because the subject of the sentence is the word *you*, which is a seed noun; also, the verb is active in each sentence. The following paragraph uses *you* as the subject of each sentence.

EXAMPLE

3. To be a good interviewer, you must charm the person you're interviewing. Use all of your human-relations skills. Smile. Talk about them, rather than about yourself. Begin with a little chitchat and express interest and curiosity. Build rapport with friendly, intriguing questions such as, "In your opinion, what is the real story here?" You might also ask for their secrets of success or fame. To be the kind of interviewer that everyone wants to talk to, you must, above all, be a good listener.

If you wish to explain step-by-step information, you can use a sequence of subjects. In the following paragraph from *Time* magazine, the subjects are circled. Notice how the last word in one sentence becomes the subject of the next sentence. When seed nouns are used as subjects, CORE CONTROL is maintained.

EXAMPLE

4. Have (you) ever wondered what happens inside a computer when a software engineer gives a computer the commands to create a new program? First, the (computer) interpreting commands one word at a time, recognizes the word PRINT and the quotation marks that follow it. The (computer) has been wired to gather up messages that appear between quotation marks and translate them, character by character, into sequences of numbers. These (numbers), in turn, are translated into a corresponding sequence of electrical signals. These (signals) are sent to an electron ''gun'' housed in the vacuum tube behind the computer's video screen. This (gun,) following the sequence of signals, fires bursts of electrons at the back side of the screen. The (electrons) strike bits of phosphor that coat the screen and energize them, lighting up a pattern of dots. These (dots) form the shape of alphabetic characters, spelling out the message: MURPHY WAS AN OPTIMIST.[1]

CORE CONTROL is an effective means of providing unity in a paragraph. Topic sentences also provide unity. Note that each of the preceding paragraphs has a specific topic sentence. A well-stated topic sentence is important to help your reader focus on your purpose.

CORE CONTROL allows you to repeat words for emphasis. If you are careful and skillful, you can repeat words often. Repeated words guide your readers by acting as signposts, showing readers where to focus their attention.

You can also use pronouns to substitute for seed nouns—Hashbacker (he)—or use the same kind of word—daisy (flower).

CORE CONTROL also includes transitional words and phrases. These words are like bridges between (and within) sentences. They help you write smoothly and connect your ideas. Transitional words and phrases help you to avoid an abrupt or choppy style. Here is a list of transitional words and phrases:

---

[1] Reprinted from ''How to Write Programs,'' by Frederick Gold, *Time*, January 1983. Reprinted by permission.

Type	Transitional Words and Phrases
Addition	at the same time, moreover, furthermore, and, likewise, also, too, in addition, next, besides, and then, nor, again, equally important, first, second, third, in the first place, finally, last
Comparison	likewise, similarly, in like manner
Contrast	yet, and yet, but, still, however, nevertheless, on the other hand, after all, on the contrary, in contrast, notwithstanding, at the same time, otherwise, in other words, beyond, here, nearby, adjacent to, opposite to, on the opposite side
Place	beyond, here, nearby, adjacent to, opposite to, on the opposite side
Purpose	for this purpose, to this end, with this object
Result	therefore, consequently, thereupon, then, hence, accordingly, thus, as a result
Summary, Repetition, Exemplification, Intensification	to sum up, on the whole, in short, in other words, to be sure, for example, in fact, to tell the truth, in brief, in summary, as I have said, that is, for instance, indeed, in any event
Time	meanwhile, in the future, ultimately, subsequently, at length, soon, in the meantime, immediately, after a few days, afterward, later, at last

Read each of the paragraphs again and <u>underline</u> the transitional words and phrases. Not every sentence is introduced by a transition, nor are transitions always necessary. Use them when you need them to make your writing flow smoothly. When you have underlined the transitions, check the end of this section for the answers.

REVIEWING FOR RESULTS

In the paragraph that follows, note the absence of a topic sentence, CORE CONTROL, and transitions. Because these elements are absent, the paragraph is hard to read and even harder to understand. To show the lack of CORE CONTROL, the subjects are circled. Notice that no unity exists among the circled subjects, so the reader has few clues as to the real meaning of the paragraph. This paragraph is an example of "textual applesauce."

The similar increase in the lack of productivity is based in part on the failure of the academic community to provide the business community with a practical, pragmatic and precise set of tools to influence and understand human motivation. To be effective in business, the individual characteristics of the people you must interact with must be dealt with constructively. Be it a secretary, a client, or a technician, these people have a different perspective and understanding of the business at hand. This difference can be an advantage if it is utilized properly. It is disastrous if it is misunderstood or mishandled. A similarly skilled understanding is needed to comprehend and influence the complex interactions of your business in relation to other businesses and the economy as a whole.

EXERCISE FOR PRACTICE

In the following paragraph, circle the subject of each sentence and <u>underline</u> the transitional words or phrases, then check your answers on page 80.

Recently, I decided to become a house husband. My wife is a dentist who enjoys her profession. As a professional writer, I chose to stay home and keep the house and care for our small son, Robbie. On cleaning day, I dug out my old tool belt with the leather multi-pouches, hammer loops, and shoulder harness. On the right side, the cleanser slips into the belt, and a Brillo pad and dustcloth fit where the page rule used to go. On the other side, the Windex, furniture polish, and squeegee stick into the hammer loop. One pocket is free for Robbie's toys, a clean diaper, powder, a cookie, and a spare bib. Now I can clean house, take care of Robbie, and start dinner without missing a step. The sale ad coupons from today's paper are half-clipped before my wife walks through the door. ''You are terrific,'' my wife greets me, and plants a big kiss on my smiling cheek. ''A good house husband is hard to find.''

Answers (page 72–75)

1. Perhaps Quarterback Hashbacker should retire from football. In the last game, he completed only four out of eighteen passes, and three were intercepted. <u>Also,</u> he was dropped twice for a loss when the defensive line charged through. Although a recent heel injury might account for a pickup of only eighteen yards rushing, he shouldn't be excused for the crucial fumbles. <u>In the end</u>, the team won by two points: a safety. Hashbacker wasn't on the field to take credit for the victory.

2. Visible products are easier to sell than services that you cannot see. <u>For example</u>, cars are easier to sell than consulting services. Buyers of visible products can judge the value and usefulness of a product quickly and easily by looking at it and by testing it. <u>On the other hand</u>, sellers of services must build trusting relationships with the buyer. They must prove that the buyer is getting good results, that the quality of the service will remain high, and that the pricing is fair. Businesses that sell services are really selling themselves. Customers demand quality in both products and services, but those who sell services face the most difficult challenge. <u>Therefore</u>, people who are focused on customer relations have the best chance of succeeding in service-based businesses.

3. To be a good interviewer, you must charm the person you're interviewing. Use all of your human-relations skills. Smile. Talk about them, rather than about yourself. Begin with a little chitchat and express interest and curiosity. Build rapport with friendly, intriguing questions such as, "<u>In your opinion</u>, what is the real story here?" You might also ask for their secrets of success or fame. To be the kind of interviewer that everyone wants to talk to, you must, <u>above all</u>, be a good listener.

4. Have you ever wondered what happens inside a computer when a software engineer gives a computer the commands to create a new program? <u>First</u>, the computer, interpreting commands one word at a time, recognizes the word PRINT and the quotation marks that follow it. The computer has been wired to gather up messages that appear between quotation marks and translate them, character by character, into sequences of numbers. These numbers, <u>in turn</u>, are translated into a corresponding sequence of electrical signals. These signals are sent to an electron "gun" housed in the vacuum tube behind the computer's video screen. This gun, following the sequence of signals, fires bursts of electrons at the back side of the screen. The electrons strike bits of phosphor that coat the screen and energize them, lighting up a pattern of dots. These dots form the shape of alphabetic characters, spelling out the message: MURPHY WAS AN OPTIMIST.[2]

CORE CONTROL is as important in paragraphs as it is in sentences. Maintain CORE CONTROL in paragraphs by relating the subjects of each sentence within a paragraph. Also, you can use transitional words and phrases to create unity and flow within paragraphs. Finally, maintain CORE CONTROL by writing a topic sentence, then relating each sentence in your paragraph to the topic sentence. These three guidelines will help you write purposeful paragraphs to meet your readers' needs.

[2]Reprinted from "How to Write Programs," by Frederick Gold, *Time*, January 1983. Reprinted by permission.

Answers (page 77)

Recently I decided to become a house husband. My wife is a dentist who enjoys her profession. As a professional writer I chose to stay home and keep the house and care for our small son, Robbie. On cleaning day I dug out my old tool belt with the leather multi-pouches, hammer loops, and shoulder harness. On the right side, the cleanser slips into the belt, and a Brillo pad and dustcloth fit where the page rule used to go. On the other side, the Windex, furniture polish, and squeegee stick into the hammer loop. One pocket is free for Robbie's toys, a clean diaper, powder, a cookie, and a spare bib. Now I can clean house, take care of Robbie, and start dinner without missing a step. The sale ad coupons from today's paper are half-clipped before my wife walks through the door. "You are terrific," my wife greets me, and plants a big kiss on my smiling cheek. "A good house husband is hard to find."

SECTION 5

WATCH OUT FOR WEED WORDS

WHAT IS A WEED WORD?

A **weed word** is any word used as a subject of a sentence that is *not* a seed noun. Many weed words are called abstract nouns. **Abstract nouns** name concepts — such as *fondness, secret, fate,* or *respect.* Weed words do not create clear visual pictures for readers, because they are feelings and ideas rather than concrete objects. Weed words do not have substance or occupy space as seed nouns do. Readers can understand your message much faster when they can see a clear picture in their minds.

Use weed words as subjects in only twenty percent of your sentences. When you don't overuse them, they provide variety, and you can use them to express broader, more abstract ideas. For this reason, many topic sentences use weed words as subjects.

EXAMPLES

The *examination* of the jury was done by the judge.

It is evident that the students are upset.

The *error* was made by me.

This means that you are correct.

The *whiteness* of the sand hurt our eyes.

EXERCISE FOR PRACTICE

In the following sentences, <u>underline</u> the subject, then decide whether the subject is a seed noun or an abstract noun — a seed word or a weed word. Put an **S** on the line if the subject is a seed word and a **W** on the line if the subject is a weed word. Check your answers at the end of this section.

_____ 1. The bolts are made of plastic.

_____ 2. The video store has extra copies of most movies.

_____ 3. This means that the flight is canceled.

_____ 4. The average person thinks he isn't.—*Larry Lorenzoni*

_____ 5. Bicycling is good exercise.

_____ 6. This problem is confusing.

_____ 7. It is your job to disagree.

_____ 8. I am too busy to have time for anything important.

_____ 9. Education has so much to learn.

_____ 10. The students liked the strange instructor.

_____ 11. Most of the future lies ahead.—*Denny Crum*

_____ 12. The new computer was difficult to use.

_____ 13. We will have a rain dance tonight, weather permitting.—*George Carlin*

_____ 14. Mitzi's laughter rang through the building.

_____ 15. The instructions were sent by fax.

FOUR KINDS OF WEED WORDS

Not all weed words are abstract nouns. Some come from other parts of speech such as verbs, adjectives, and signal words. These words are changed into noun forms and used as subjects.

EXAMPLE

A reduction in the work force is expected.

Reduction is a noun that was originally a verb (to reduce). Weed words are divided into four categories: (1) nouns created from verbs, (2) nouns created from modifiers, (3) nouns created from signal words, and (4) abstract nouns.

Nouns Created from Verbs

EXAMPLES

Noise *reduction* improved worker efficiency.
Ice *skating* requires strong ankles.
A *conclusion* was reached by the committee.
The *implementation* of the policy was immediate.

The subjects of the sentences in the examples are used as nouns, but they were originally verbs. Each comes from a basic verb form called an **infinitive**.

Noun	Verb (Infinitive)
reduction	to reduce
skating	to skate
conclusion	to conclude
implementation	to implement

Verbs are more effective and more helpful to the reader when they are used as verbs. The following sentences show you how to rewrite each example sentence above so that the nouns now used as subjects can be used as verbs. When you change subjects into verbs, you need a new subject to replace the verb. In other words, you must identify *who* is acting. If a subject is needed, we will use, *we.*

EXAMPLES

Noise *reduction* improved worker efficiency.
The *workers* improved their efficiency when the noise level was reduced.

> This sentence is longer than the original sentence, but *workers* is a visual noun and *improved* is an active verb. *Was reduced* is a passive verb phrase used as part of a dependent core. This sentence is more direct and avoids sounding like "businessese."

Ice *skating* requires strong ankles.
This sentence is a good sentence as it is.

> When you choose subjects that are *not* seed nouns, action verbs that end in *-ing* are good choices as subjects. In twenty percent of your sentences you can choose subjects that are not seed nouns, and your style will remain clear. By occasionally choosing abstract subjects or nouns created from verbs, you provide variety for your reader.

A *conclusion* was reached by the committee.
The *committee* reached a conclusion.

> This sentence is shorter and the verb is active rather than passive. You can also say, "The committee concluded that..."

The *implementation* of the policy was immediate.
We implemented the policy immediately.

> This sentence is shorter, the verb is active, and the subject *we* tells the reader who performed the action. The verb *implemented* is stronger as a verb than it was as a noun (*implementation*).

From these examples, you can see that *most* sentences can be improved by using seed nouns as subjects followed by active verbs. If you follow the Twenty-Eighty Rule (to use seed nouns and active or linking verbs in eighty percent of your sentences), you will not have any trouble with nouns and verbs, and your writing will be clear and concise. When you use weed words as subjects (the other twenty percent of the time), choose nouns created from verbs, because they are somewhat visual.

EXERCISE FOR PRACTICE

In the following sentences, each underlined subject is a noun created from a verb. Rewrite the sentences using a seed noun and an active or linking verb. Sentences can often be written in several ways. The answers reflect the best choice for each sentence. When you have finished, check the end of this section for the answers.

1. Help was given by the City Council to the street people.

2. A decision was made to buy a new postage meter.

3. The adoption of the puppy by the children was immediate.

4. Requirements for new pets are love and care.

5. Clear thinking is hard work.

6. Changes were made in the final draft.

NOUNS CREATED FROM MODIFIERS

EXAMPLES

Her *honesty* was questionable.
The *peacefulness* of the valley was pleasant.
Nothing happened at the staff meeting.
Bilbo's *competence* was welcomed by his manager.
The *quickness* of the lifeguard's reaction saved the swimmer's life.

Nouns in the sentences above are created from modifiers, usually adjectives. In the following examples, the sentences have been rewritten, replacing the modifiers with seed nouns.

EXAMPLES

Her *honesty* was questionable.
We questioned her honesty.

> The word *honesty* becomes the completer. *Questionable* becomes the
> verb, *questioned*, and the sentence now has a seed noun as the subject.
> The verb *questioned* is active, so the sentence has CORE CONTROL.

The *peacefulness* of the valley was pleasant.
The peaceful *valley* was pleasant.

> *Valley* becomes the subject, *peacefulness* becomes the modifier *peaceful*.
> *Was* is the linking verb, and *pleasant* is the completer.

Nothing happened at the staff meeting.
The staff *meeting* was unproductive.

> This sentence uses *meeting* rather than *nothing* as the subject.
> However, ''Nothing happened at the staff meeting'' is not a bad
> sentence as it is, because the idea is expressed clearly. We are simply
> showing you here how to shift to CORE CONTROL.

Bilbo's *competence* was welcomed by his manager.
Bilbo's *manager* welcomed his competence.

> *Manager* is a seed noun, *welcomed* becomes an active verb, and
> *competence* becomes the completer. This sentence uses CORE
> CONTROL.

The *quickness* of the lifeguard's reaction saved the swimmer's life.
The *lifeguard* reacted quickly, and saved the swimmer's life.

> *Lifeguard* should be the subject because it is a seed noun.
> *Reacted* becomes the active verb, and *quickly* becomes an adverb.

90

EXERCISE FOR PRACTICE

In the following sentences, each underlined subject is a noun created from a modifier. Rewrite the sentence using a seed noun and an active or linking verb. Sentences can often be written in several ways. These answers reflect the best choice for each sentence. When you have finished, check the end of this section for answers.

1. The <u>seriousness</u> of the crime was considered by the jury.

2. <u>Nothing</u> appeared in the X-ray of Bill's head.

3. Hecuba's <u>beauty</u> was noticed by Silas.

4. The <u>sadness</u> in Arlo's voice caused Cassandra to weep.

5. <u>Each</u> of the forms was long and confusing.

6. Your <u>kindness</u> is much appreciated.

NOUNS CREATED FROM VAGUE PRONOUNS

EXAMPLES

This means that the project is complete.
It is possible to finish the report by Tuesday.
There are two keys in the drawer.

The vague pronouns *it, this,* and *there* used as subjects in the sentences above are seldom good choices. Vague pronouns act as subjects, but they do not create a picture. They cause confusion for the reader because they do not refer to specific words in the sentence. Using *it, this,* or *there* as subjects is an easy habit to change, once you realize that you are using them. Limit vague pronouns to occasional use for variety or emphasis—for example, ''This won't do!'' In the following examples, the sentences have been rewritten replacing the vague pronouns with seed nouns.

EXAMPLES

This *signature* means that the project is complete.
> In the first sentence, we do not know what *This* refers to. In the second sentence, we define what *This* means. *This* becomes a modifier of the subject, *signature*. *Means* is the linking verb.

We may be able to finish the report by Tuesday.
> Use a seed noun as a subject (*we*), and let the verb convey the doubt.

Two *keys* are in the drawer. OR *You* will find two keys in the drawer.
> The word *There* is not actually the subject, because *there* is never the subject of a sentence. However, it is in italics as the subject because it is often mistaken for a subject. *Keys* is the true subject. You can leave off the word *there* at the beginning of most sentences. Use the word *there* in a sentence when you mean *in that place*—for example, ''The key is over there.''

EXERCISE FOR PRACTICE

In the following sentences, each underlined subject is a vague pronoun. Rewrite the sentence using a seed noun and an active or linking verb. Sentences can often be written in several ways. These answers reflect the best choice for each sentence. When you have finished, check the end of this section for the answers.

1. <u>This</u> is an important piece of the puzzle.

2. <u>There</u> were several people waiting in line.

3. <u>It</u> is essential that the bundles be delivered on time.

4. <u>This</u> indicates that the operators lack training.

5. <u>There</u> are many reasons why Ralphie should stay here.

6. <u>It</u> means that we can leave early.

ABSTRACT NOUNS

EXAMPLES

The *elements* of the formula were complex.
The *nature* of the beast is unpredictable.
Comedy is nothing to laugh at.
Certain *parts* of the system are difficult to use.

Abstract nouns are nouns that describe an idea or a feeling. They may be included in a sentence, but avoid using them as subjects. Sometimes they can be edited out without losing any of the meaning of the sentence. Choose visual nouns rather than abstract nouns whenever possible. In the following examples, the sentences above have been rewritten using seed nouns as subjects.

EXAMPLES

The *elements* of the formula were complex.
    The *formula* was complex
        OR
    The *formula* contains complex elements.
    Formula should be the subject, and the verb can be either linking or active.
    In the first rewritten example, the word *elements* is left out.

The *nature* of the beast is unpredictable.
    The *beast* is unpredictable.
    The completer, *unpredictable,* implies the nature of the beast. *Nature* can be edited out without changing the meaning of the sentence.

EXAMPLES

Comedy is nothing to laugh at.
> This sentence is okay as it is. You could also say, "You should take comedy seriously," but then the humor of the statement is lost. This sentence makes good use of an abstract subject. When you choose abstract subjects, try to keep your sentences short and to the point.

My *opinion* may have changed, but not the fact that I am right.
> *I* may change my opinion, but I am still right.
> *I* is a seed noun. *Opinion* becomes the completer. In the second core, *I* is also the subject. You can leave out *the fact that*.

EXERCISE FOR PRACTICE

In the following sentences, each underlined subject is an abstract noun. Rewrite the sentence using a seed noun and an active or linking verb. Sentences can often be written in several ways. These answers reflect the best choice for each sentence. When you have finished, check the end of this section for the answers.

1. My favorite <u>way</u> to end a game is by winning.

2. A <u>purpose</u> for writing is important.

3. A <u>variation</u> in the code caused the crew to delay the project.

4. My <u>objective</u> is to save the world while still leading a pleasant life.

5. The <u>opinion</u> stated by the judge was final.

6. All <u>aspects</u> of the grading system were discussed by the students.

REVIEWING FOR RESULTS

In the following sentences, <u>underline</u> the subject, then fill in the blank with letters from the following list to indicate what kind of noun the subject is. Check your answers at the end of this section.

S   Seed noun
V   Noun created from a verb
M   Noun created from a modifier
VP   Noun created from a vague pronoun
A   Abstract noun

EXAMPLES

_V_ <u>Spelling</u> was my favorite subject in school.

_VP_ <u>This</u> indicates that the results are incorrect.

_A_ <u>Exceptions</u> are made every day.

_M_ Her <u>inexperience</u> shows.

_S_ The <u>shoe</u> fits.

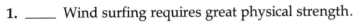

1. ____ Wind surfing requires great physical strength.
2. ____ Inflation is a stab in the buck.
3. ____ The correctness of the decision was evident.
4. ____ Johnny Appleseed used CORE CONTROL.
5. ____ It is evident that the new designer is well qualified.
6. ____ There are two soldering irons on the shelf.
7. ____ Anything is good if it is made of chocolate.
8. ____ Words can never express what words can never express.
9. ____ Her expressiveness helped her win the acting award.
10. ____ The auditors approved our request for more funds.
11. ____ Forecasting is difficult, especially when it involves the future.
12. ____ This indicates a change in direction.

EXERCISE FOR PRACTICE

Rewrite the following sentences using CORE CONTROL. Change the weed words in the subject positions to seed nouns. Use active or linking verbs. When you are finished, check the end of this section for the answers. Sentences can often be written in several ways.

1. The conclusion that they have reached regarding the new book design is that it will probably decrease the cost of publication.

2. The serious nature of the problem suggests that a committee should be formed to investigate.

3. Your interpreting the final results in the summary section would mean that the data could be processed by us much faster.

4. If operating changes are required, additional training will be needed for the operators.

5. It was evident that his reaction to the plan was positive.

6. There is a good chance that the announcement of the campus survey results sponsored by the Academic Committee will probably be delayed until after Student Council elections.

EXERCISE FOR PRACTICE (Continued)

7. There are several reasons for changing the production schedule, according to my supervisor.

8. The most difficult tongue twister in the English language is considered by many people to be, "The sixth sick sheikh's sixth sheep's sick."

9. In the event that requirements are changed for the position, applicants should be informed by the Employment Office.

10. My theory is that it is impossible to prove anything; however, I am unable to prove it at this point in time.

ANSWERS FOR SECTION 5

Answers (page 84)

- S 1. The <u>bolts</u> are made of plastic.
- S 2. The video <u>store</u> has extra copies of most movies.
- W 3. <u>This</u> means that the flight is canceled.
- S 4. The average <u>person</u> thinks he isn't.—*Larry Lorenzoni*
- W 5. <u>Bicycling</u> is good exercise.
- W 6. This <u>problem</u> is confusing.
- W 7. <u>It</u> is your job to disagree.
- S 8. <u>I</u> am too busy to have time for anything important.
- W 9. <u>Education</u> has so much to learn.
- S 10. The <u>students</u> liked the strange instructor.
- W 11. <u>Most</u> of the future lies ahead.—*Denny Crum*
- S 12. The new <u>computer</u> was difficult to use.
- S 13. <u>We</u> will have a rain dance tonight, weather permitting.—*George Carlin*
- W 14. Mitzi's <u>laughter</u> rang through the building.
- S 15. The <u>instructions</u> were sent by fax.

NOTE: To determine whether the subjects above are seed words or weed words, ask yourself if you can see or touch them. If you can, they are seed words. In a sentence 5, *bicycling* is an action; however, a *bicycle* is a seed noun.

Answers (page 87)

When you have completed this exercise, look at your own letters, reports, or school papers to see if you use nouns created from verbs as subjects. Where possible, change your sentences so that you are using consistent CORE CONTROL.

1. The <u>City Council</u> helped the street people.
2. <u>They</u> decided to buy a new postage meter.
3. The <u>children</u> adopted the puppy immediately.
4. New <u>pets</u> require love and care.
5. (This sentence is okay as it is.)
6. <u>I</u> changed the final draft.
    OR
   The final <u>draft</u> required changes.

Answers (page 90)

1. The <u>seriousness</u> of the crime was considered by the jury.

   The <u>jury</u> considered the seriousness of the crime.

   > or

   The <u>jury</u> considered the serious crime.

2. <u>Nothing</u> appeared in the X-ray of Bill's head.

   The <u>X-ray</u> of Bill's head showed nothing.

3. Hecuba's <u>beauty</u> was noticed by Silas.

   <u>Silas</u> noticed Hecuba's beauty.

4. The <u>sadness</u> in Arlo's voice caused Cassandra to weep.

   <u>Cassandra</u> wept at the sadness in Arlo's voice.

5. <u>Each</u> of the forms was long and confusing.

   Each <u>form</u> was long and confusing.

6. Your <u>kindness</u> is much appreciated.

   <u>I</u> appreciate your kindness.

Answers (page 92)

1. <u>This</u> is an important piece of the puzzle.
This <u>piece</u> of the puzzle is important.

2. <u>There</u> were several people waiting in line.
Several <u>people</u> were waiting in line.

3. <u>It</u> is essential that the bundles be delivered on time.
The <u>bundles</u> must be delivered on time.

4. <u>This</u> indicates that the operators lack training.
This <u>report</u> indicates that the operators lack training.
The <u>operators</u> are making errors because they lack training.

5. <u>There</u> are many reasons why Ralphie should stay here.
<u>Ralphie</u> should stay here for many reasons
OR
<u>Ralphie</u> should stay here because...

6. <u>It</u> means that we can leave early.
<u>We</u> can leave early because...
OR
<u>We</u> are finished, so we can leave early.

Vague pronouns are not vague when they have an **antecedent**, a word in the sentence that identifies what the pronoun means. For example:

EXAMPLE

The computer is broken. It was sent out for repairs.

The word *it* refers to the computer. In this instance, the word *it* is used correctly. In the sentence, "This wire leads to the engine," *this* modifies *wire*. The word *this* is used correctly as a modifier. Pronouns are vague only when they do not have clear referents.

Answers (page 94)

1. My favorite <u>way</u> to end a game is by winning.
   <u>I</u> prefer to end a game by winning.

2. A <u>purpose</u> for writing is important.
   <u>You</u> should have a purpose for writing.

3. A <u>variation</u> in the code caused the crew to delay the project.
   The <u>crew</u> delayed the project because of a variation in the code.

4. My <u>objective</u> is to save the world while still leading a pleasant life.
   <u>I</u> plan to save the world, while still leading a pleasant life.

5. The <u>opinion</u> stated by the judge was final.
   The <u>judge</u> stated his final opinion.

6. All <u>aspects</u> of the grading system were discussed by the students.
   The <u>students</u> discussed all aspects of the grading system.

Answers (page 95)

1. __V__ Wind <u>surfing</u> requires great physical strength.
2. __A__ <u>Inflation</u> is a stab in the buck.
3. __M__ The <u>correctness</u> of the decision was evident.
4. __S__ <u>Johnny Appleseed</u> used CORE CONTROL.
5. __VP__ <u>It</u> is evident that the new designer is well qualified.
6. __VP__ <u>There</u> are two soldering irons on the shelf.
7. __M__ <u>Anything</u> is good if it is made of chocolate.
8. __A__ <u>Words</u> can never express what words can never express.
9. __M__ Her <u>expressiveness</u> helped her win the acting award.
10. __S__ The <u>auditors</u> approved our request for more funds.
11. __V__ <u>Forecasting</u> is difficult, especially when it involves the future.
12. __VP__ <u>This</u> indicates a change in direction.

Answers (page 96)

1. The conclusion that they have reached regarding the new book design is that it will probably decrease the cost of publication.

   They concluded that the new book design will probably decrease the publication cost.

2. The serious nature of the problem suggests that a committee should be formed to investigate.

   They should form a committee to investigate the serious problem.

3. Your interpreting the test results in the summary section would mean that the data could be processed by us much faster.

   If you interpret the test results in the summary section, we could process the data much faster.

4. If operating changes are required, additional training will be needed for the operators.

   If operating changes are required, the operators will need additional training.

5. It was evident that his reaction to the plan was positive.

   Evidently he liked the plan.

6. There is a good chance that the announcement of the campus survey results sponsored by the Academic Committee will probably be delayed until after Student Council elections.

   The Academic Committee may delay the announcement of the campus survey results until after the Student Council elections.

7. There are several reasons for changing the production schedule, according to my supervisor.

   My supervisor has several reasons for changing the production schedule.

8. The most difficult tongue twister in the English language is considered by many people to be, "The sixth sick sheikh's sixth sheep's sick."

   Many people consider the most difficult tongue twister in the English language to be, "The sixth sick sheikh's sixth sheep's sick."

9. In the event that requirements are changed for the position, applicants should be informed by the Employment Office.

   If requirements for the position are changed, the Employment Office should inform the applicants.

10. My theory is that it is impossible to prove anything; however, I am unable to prove it at this point in time.

    I have a theory that nothing can be proven, but I can't prove it.

SECTION 6

PUTTING IT TOGETHER

COMPLETE DOCUMENTS

Now you are ready to move from paragraphs to complete documents: memos, letters, essays, and other written information. CORE CONTROL applies to all writing, so you can use it any time. Whether you are a student, a business person, or a beginning writer interested in self-improvement, CORE CONTROL helps you gain confidence and sail over the rough spots. This section provides three practice exercises: writing a letter, a memo, and a short essay. Each exercise provides examples. When you have completed this section, you can handle any document — long or short — with ease and skill. CORE CONTROL will be ''as easy as apple pie.''

WRITING BUSINESS MEMOS

You should now be prepared to write a business memo using the information you have learned.* Refer to the applicable sections of the book to help you practice CORE CONTROL in each exercise. Use seed nouns and active or linking verbs in eighty percent of your sentences. Circle the subject of each sentence to check your use of seed nouns.

INSTRUCTIONS: Write a memo to your manager suggesting a plan of action for improving a task or procedure in your office. Include the benefits of your plan in order to persuade him or her to act.

Example of a Well-Written Memo

TO: Lloyd Balfour
FROM: Terry Bradshaw
SUBJECT: New Computers
DATE: May 29, 1991

This week I surveyed the number of different computers and word processing systems in our department. We have twenty-seven people in our department and they are using eighteen different systems, which creates serious communication problems. As a result, we cannot share information easily and we waste time duplicating information.

I would like to suggest that we change to one system and train everyone in the department to use it. That way we can transfer information easily and we will have access to information that is already available.

May we meet before our next staff meeting to discuss this idea? I have several suggestions for possible systems that would not be too expensive to install. Our old systems could be donated to local schools.

---

*For several excellent references on formatting and writing memos, letters, and reports, refer to *Better Business Writing* by Sue Brock; *Technical Writing in the Corporate World* by Herman Estrin and Nobert Elliot; and *Writing Fitness* by Jack Swenson. Crisp Publications.

WRITING BUSINESS LETTERS

INSTRUCTIONS: Write a letter of refusal to an organization that has asked you to volunteer your time or a service. Tone is important in this letter, so be honest, and say no nicely. Offer other ideas, or suggest people who can help. Circle the subject of each sentence to check your use of CORE CONTROL.

Example of a Well-Written Business Letter

May 29, 1991

328 Greensboro Way
Charleston, SC 93200

Scouts of America
407 Main St.
Charleston, SC 93200

Dear Mr. Goldman:

Thank you for inviting me to speak at the Annual Scouts of America Awards Banquet. Although I enjoy working with my own small group of scouts, I am quite shy and am very uncomfortable in any public speaking situation. (Once when asked to pray over the offering at my church, I fainted in front of the entire congregation.)

If you would like help setting up for the banquet, I am available. Also, my fellow Scout Leader, Socrates Ames, is a member of Toastmasters. He may be able to help you. His number is 423-7651.

I have enjoyed my four years as a Scout Leader. With two more sons ready to enter Scouts, I hope to be with you for quite some time. (You) Please let me know if I can help with the banquet.

All the best

Frank Lee Mideer

Frank Lee Mideer

WRITING SHORT ESSAYS

INSTRUCTIONS: Write a short essay (three or four paragraphs) describing CORE CONTROL and how you can use it to write clearly. Circle the subject of each sentence to assure CORE CONTROL.

NOTE: The word you is often omitted when making a polite request or giving a command. When you is omitted, sentences begin with a verb. **Example:** Help me with this problem. Although you is omitted, it is still the "understood" subject of the sentence. In the essay below the understood you is in parenthesis.

Example of a Well-Written Essay

CLEAR WRITING

(*You*) Imagine you're the editor, not the writer of this piece. You are seeing it for the first time, and your job is to carve out the best of what is here. As an editor, you are not looking for textbook English, but writing with strength and drive. You do not want to change your writing style, only to tighten and sharpen what you have. Sentences should be written with CORE CONTROL, and they should be interesting. You begin by crossing out extra words, without regret. You kill extra adverbs and adjectives. If the subject and verb are solid, you do not need extra modifiers.

You move from one sentence to the next. Do the sentences follow logically? You ask yourself, "What is the point this person is making?" Do transitions guide you from one idea to the next?

You begin a new paragraph. The topic sentence tells you what to expect. As you continue to look for CORE CONTROL, you spot sentences that begin with "It," "This," or "There," and your red pencil strikes with deadly precision. Sentences that begin with "This means" or "There are" sound dull. You find just the right seed noun to make the subject come alive and dance before your eyes. Also, you make sure that the subject of each sentence in the paragraph relates to the subjects of the other sentences.

In summary, you are in charge of your writing. (*You*) Get tough on yourself as a writer by becoming your own editor. Soon you will use CORE CONTROL easily. Transitions will seem natural, and you will quickly catch those words and phrases that do not add to your message. (*You*) Be persistent, and (*you*) be sure to reward yourself as you see improvement.

NOTES

NOTES

NOTES

NOTES

NOTES

NOTES

NOTES

NOTES

OVER 150 BOOKS AND 35 VIDEOS AVAILABLE IN THE 50-MINUTE SERIES

50-Minute Series Books and Videos Subject Areas . . .

Management
Training
Human Resources
Customer Service and Sales Training
Communications
Small Business and Financial Planning
Creativity
Personal Development
Wellness
Adult Literacy and Learning
Career, Retirement and Life Planning

Other titles available from Crisp Publications in these categories

Crisp Computer Series
The Crisp Small Business & Entrepreneurship Series
Quick Read Series
Management
Personal Development
Retirement Planning